T0160507

TRANSFORMATION

TRANSFORMATION

Speaking Spirit to Spirit

DR. JERRY ROBERSON

Carpenter's Son Publishing

Transformation: Speaking Spirit to Spirit

Published by Clovercroft Publishing, Franklin, Tennessee

Scripture quotations from The Authorized (King James) Version. Rights in the Authorized Version in the United Kingdom are vested in the Crown. Reproduced by permission of the Crown's patentee, Cambridge University Press

Edited by Lapiz Digital Services

Cover Design by Sarah Thurstenson

Interior Design by Adept Content Solutions

Printed in the United States of America

ISBN   978-1-948484-97-8

CONTENTS

DEDICATION AND ACKNOWLEDGEMENTS

This book is dedicated to all of those that are seekers of light. May you be inspired to look, listen, learn, reflect, filter—rinse and repeat. May the elasticity of the content in this book stretch you, connect you, and free you.

To all of those that prayed for me before I knew how to pray for myself. Thank you.

To my parents, Kirby Roberson and Dorothy Roberson. In the most humble of ways, the two of you equipped each of us to face the world and survive. You put some "really good stuff" in us. I am eternally grateful.

To my most cherished gift from God, my daughter Jerrilyn. It is an honor to be your father. You inspire me. It never gets too bad for us to talk about it. May you be motivated. May your heart be warmed. May your spirit be nourished. I love you with all that I am.

To every single member of my tribe—Jesse, Ada, Wilbut, Dorothy, Carolyn, Brenda, Kirby Jr. "Buddy", Fredric, Jonathan, Bredric, Kiedric, Cherish, Nerlande, Rhonda, Adalyn

Joy, Jasmine, Nisera, Jewel, Cardell, Darlene, Deloris, Alvina, and Carlos. In your varied and unique ways, each of you have deposited things in me that are simply beyond measure. I hope to make you proud.

To the Green Family Tree. I am standing on your shoulders, for I could not be nor share from my heart were it not for what was created by my grandparents—Henry Green and Ada (Morris-Jackson). May God bless each and every single one of you. As Mama Ada often said, "Jesus Please!"

To 'Da Brothers'—Carlos, Guillermo (Sempai), Darryl, Howard, Thad, Buz, Torrance, Terence, Julian, Bryan, Brisco, Victor, Jackie (honorary sister), my peeps in Baker Quarters, and countless others. It is probably a mistake to call names, but fellas, know that I am grateful to each of you. I am because you are. To Golden Rule #311 and Iota Mu Sigma, know that you all don't see me often, but I am and forever will be connected. May the Grand Architect keep you. May God forever sustain you. May the light eternal forever light your path as you traverse the limitations of time.

FOREWORD

W hat is a man?
Created in the image of God, yes, but unpredictable nonetheless.

No one was more surprised than I when I received a call from my assistant one day informing me that our TEDx honoree and speaker wanted to share the stage.

I protested immediately!

"The TEDx talk is delivered by only one person," I replied. "You can't share the stage. We select specific humans, based on their audition message."

She hesitated.

There was silence on the line for a long time.

"He wants to bring his dog," she insisted. "He wants his dog on stage!"

I remember telling her no, again, and that there was no way that anyone of our speakers could bring an animal on stage as it was surely a violation of the TEDx rules.

Within seconds, she texted me an image of the dog.

When you watch Dr. Jerry's TEDx talk that he delivered at the Marriott Hotel in Flower Mound Texas, you'll see why I had no choice but to say yes. His plans are directed by God, his steps ordered by the Almighty. How can one argue with that? Chip made an appearance on stage that day and wedged his way into the hearts of thousands. Like the words within this book, his TEDx talk offers redemption. How do we recover from the worst tragedies of our lives? How do we continue to see hope when it feels as if there is none?

The book you hold in your hands is a blessing. It is a book of transformation written by one of the most prolific writers of our generation. Leaders, organizations, and individuals seek his counsel and wisdom, yet he delivers it with ease and humility.

In my years of working with world changers, including world leaders, presidents, kings of nations, celebrity pastors, and CEOs, I have not encountered such a great writer as this. It is a rare moment indeed to receive a manuscript from a thought leader whose words seem inspired by divine intervention.

When I read it, I realized that not only would I equip this world changer to speak on a global stage but that his words would impact generations.

This is a book that is more than just a book, and one you will want to pass on to someone you love when you're finished. After decades of reading books by inspiring speakers, CEOs, and authors, this one took me aback. It's reminiscent of C.S. Lewis, who seemed to create God-given words written from the point of view of angels.

Without question you're here for a reason, already engaged in these pages, even if you're not sure why.

What can you expect to receive?

Life.

He writes:

Transformation is a process. Breathing life into that which is dead is profoundly difficult to gauge—mildly stated, it is simply hard to measure. As is the case more often than not "the truth" is revealed in tiny granules that are sustainable over time.

As the author shares his own stories and observations, you'll no doubt internalize them for your own daily walk.

God has a plan for you and this journey you're on, and no matter where you are in life, there's always more to learn.

In the author's own words, "As you read on, choose to search for liberation and not limitation."

You were created to love.

Tammy Kling
CEO The Conversation
OnFire Books

HOW TO USE THIS BOOK

One of the most powerful ways to learn, reflect, and make sense of our lives is through reading and journaling. This book presents readers with both rich narrative and a platform for journaling.

The book is written in a style that is intended to be an easy initial read. However, know that the content is inward to initiate thought; therefore, there will more than likely be an internal solicitation for the reader to revisit the material. The reader is encouraged to look inward and do a self-assessment about the degree to which the material resonates with their unique internal dataset. This process of reflection will stimulate an internal dialogue. The reader is challenged to use the prompting questions to facilitate the internal dialogue. Listen to and ponder the discussions, as there will be many. Readers are challenged to look for opportunities to learn more about themselves.

Readers are encouraged to journal extensively. Both writing and rereading journal entries allow the journal keeper to document thinking, to track changes and review observations, and to examine assumptions and so gain fresh perspectives and insights over past events. Notice that over time, the responses to the questions will more than likely change.

All are encouraged to reread and repeat all of the aforementioned.

CHAPTER 1

INTRODUCTION—THE SEVEN DAYS
OF HELL: DISCOVERING ALIGNMENT

Transformation is a process. Breathing life into that which is dead is profoundly difficult to gauge—mildly stated, it is simply hard to measure. As is the case more often than not, "the truth" is revealed in tiny granules that are sustainable over time. For the believer, the perseverance of truth is essential as the time and the visible substantive justification are forensically elusive.

As I reference the sacred volume of the Christian body of faith—the Bible—know that it doesn't matter what you profess to be. Your chosen faith journey or faith community is not relevant, as the content of this book is not about religion. It is about the connection to the Source of all. It is about expansion. Inserting the controlling parameters of categories limits and does not liberate. As you read on, choose to search for liberation and not limitation. You were created to love. Love transcends all parameters, boundaries, and limitations.

Pain and pondering come from the past. Power is in connection with the present. Prosperity is grounded in the promises of God or that which is greater than yourself. You can call it whatever you like, but know that there is something out there greater than yourself. With that being said, have you ever had a week when things went bad? I had the week from hell. Validation of this point came after a long and difficult week filled with pain, loss, and lessons. The week went like this.

Day 1.
The marriage that I'd been in for a few years had finally reached the point of no return. Early on that Monday morning, I decided that the marriage was over and that I had to find a place to live—a new space, a place that would be my new home. I did find a new apartment and began working toward moving.

My goal was to be completely moved out of the home that had become like hell's den to my new place, my new chapter, my space of healing, the place that would become my refuge—a place of transformation, Jerusalem—a place of peace. I initiated the steps to move—secured the apartment, got a storage space to hold some of my things, and put together a crew of my buddies to help me get my items moved to the new space. By the end of day 1, all bases to make the move go smoothly had been coordinated. Next was the packing. I would start that on day 2.

Day 2.
Day 2 was the day of death. Three people that I'd known since I was a kid all passed away within thirty-six hours.

There was a young lady who lived in the old neighborhood, actually on the same street, where I grew up. She was the prettiest and the finest girl that I'd ever seen. She was older than me. But I remember looking at her and thinking "she is truly one of God's finest creations." She had beautiful green eyes and blemish-free caramel skin. She wore the original pair of Daisy Dukes—really, really short shorts. Her extended family had houses at or near both ends of the street that we all lived on. Every day, she and other members of her family would walk up and down the street between the shared abodes. Did I mention that she wore short shorts? Anyway, as she blossomed into adulthood, this young lady was diagnosed with some debilitating disease that she would spend the rest of her life fighting.

Well, finally, she lost the fight. She died at the age of 85.

Some of the most impactful people in a young person's life—well, I'll say in my life as a youth, it was my Sunday School teacher. He was a gentleman, a humble servant who was gifted at fielding the crazy questions of obnoxious teens. My church friends and I asked him all sorts of questions. He never shied away from the questions. Nothing was off limits. He often said, "Ask me anything you want. If I don't have the answer, I will go and find the answer." He always found a way to make the lesson of the day relevant for us kids. Well, I received word that he passed in the calm of the night. His wife said that he had eaten his favorite meal—fried catfish, homemade escalloped potatoes, and mustard greens. She said that he had complained about having had issues with his asthma earlier on that day. We all knew about his asthma. She said that when he came home from work, he seemed to have been more tired than usual. She said that he usually would get completely exhausted after a bad asthma day, so after dinner, he took a shower and went to bed early. When she went in to check on him, he was nonresponsive. She called 911, and the ambulance got to the house in about seven minutes. Upon their arrival, it was determined that he had already passed.

On that same evening, I got a call from a cousin telling me that my uncle had a stroke and that they didn't know how much longer he would be alive. This was *my* uncle. Of all of my parents' brothers, he was the one that I was closest to. When I was a kid, during the summers, I worked with him. He was a general contractor, but his specialty was swimming pools. He traveled all over the country building amazing swimming pools for all sorts of people. His work ethic was unreal. We'd start the day at 5:00 a.m. and finish by 7:00 or so in the evening. He was always very pleasant, constantly wearing a bit of a smile on his face. He taught you things by asking you questions. Your answer would dictate the direction and the depth of the rest of the conversation. We spent many hours talking sports, primarily football and boxing. He introduced me to our fraternity and was a key influencer on that journey. He was a great father and husband. He was a great person. Well, on this day, he too transitioned from this life to be with the Lord.

There you have it, three very dear people to me, dead within a thirty-six-hour window. Funeral arrangements were made for all the three. My uncle, my childhood friend, and my Sunday school teacher would all be buried on the upcoming Saturday. Two of my sisters and I agreed to drive home together to pay our final respects, so we started making plans to travel so that we could attend all three funerals.

Day 3.

I had been self-employed for several years. My company was centered around a number of programs that provided services in the discipline of maternal and child health. My service to these groups was to perform program evaluations. I had been doing the program evaluation work for almost twelve years. Well, the federal government changed a policy that had a direct and immediate impact on my entire clientele. There was a change in the law regarding contracted service providers in these programs. All of the sites that were paying me and several others to do program evaluation would no longer be allowed to use federal resources to pay subcontractors. Basically, all of my clients terminated contracts with program evaluators and other subcontracted providers. So on that one day, I lost about $200K of incoming revenue. In essence, my company went belly up because of the policy change.

Day 4.

Day 4 was moving day. It wasn't exactly pleasant. My estranged wife was very upset, as was I. I was confused at her reason for being upset. She didn't want me. She was always unhappy about something. It was as though she wanted to keep me so that we could both be in a state of misery, in a living state of death. I chose to live. Maybe that is why she was upset. We had exhausted all possible means for reconciliation. The problems within the marriage had a life of their own. There were so many issues, I won't bore you with the details, but understand that tension was in the air. We were like focused vessels filled with cargo headed in different directions.

My guys showed up at about 7:30 that morning, and we started loading the trucks. It was a long day. Moving might be one of the most dreaded and frustrating necessities. Box by box, we packed up the life that I'd known for several years. We carried the remains of my existence in a bunch of boxes and neatly stacked them in the back of a moving truck. Attention was given to the silence as my friends kept moving.

My estranged wife stirred the tension with cold and glaring eyes. The achy sound of the rolling dolly carrying the weight and contents of my life continued to roll. It was a long day—constant movement. By the end, I sat in my new apartment. As dusk settled in, the darkness brought forth the reality of the moment. On some level, the tension that had been plaguing me quite some time in a troubled marriage had given way to sheer numbness from the day's labor. Darkness took over the apartment and eliminated the shadows of the pain of the last several months. I didn't have electricity because I didn't have the money to get the move fully executed and get the lights turned on. Nonetheless, I sat in stillness, in the dark for several hours. Completely exhausted, finally I fell asleep on an air mattress.

Day 5.

With the rising of the sun—the dawn of a new day—for me, this was the start of a new era. I began by going back to my old home to pick up the remaining small things that are always the last things to go in a move. That time was both solemn and liberating all at once. I knew when I closed the front door that this, for all intents and purposes, was the conclusion of that chapter of my life.

After making it back to my apartment, I had to make a number of decisions as to what was going to stay at the apartment and what was going to storage. On this day, I did not have help, so the entire day was an intense reflection exercise, as I sorted through the contents of boxes that were obviously hurriedly packed. It was all there, work materials, personal care items, workout equipment, pots and pans, clothes, my Bible, etc.

There was my life—lying on the floor of my apartment in complete disarray. As the sunlight of the day started moving westward in the direction of a setting sun, I went to check my mailbox. Aha, a good thing! One of my checks had arrived. I immediately got to the bank and made the deposit. I paid the fees online to get the lights turned on, but because it was late on a Friday evening, the lights would not be eligible to turn on until the following Tuesday morning, so three more days without lights.

That evening, my sisters and I would be leaving to travel to Louisiana to attend the three funerals. Before heading over to meet up with them, I stopped at the mall. There was a purchase that I'd decided to make months earlier. There were these sunglasses that I wanted. The glasses were $200. Needless to say, that was a big purchase for me. The glasses were really nice, but more important was what they represented. They were emblematic of my new outlook on life.

Have you ever wanted to change your perspective or outlook? The physical object would be a great reminder of that for me.

I was late meeting up with my sisters, but I had to get the glasses before we got on the road.

Day 6.
This was the day of funerals. It was a time for celebrating the lives of those that we loved. Of course, there were moments of sorrow and sadness. There is always something special about these gatherings. Although the paying of

final respects is the point of focus, in so many ways, this is a golden time when all reflect on their own lives and a time to see people that perhaps you have not seen in years. I saw people at all three funerals whom I had not seen in twenty years.

In a strange sort of way, this day was very comforting. It was a reminder of the mortal nature of this human experience. We are all born and we shall all die. Giving what had been happening in my life as of late, I had deep thoughts of my past, my present, and, most importantly, what was next for me. There are few things more sobering than death. Everything else is pretty negotiable. The rest of the day was spent driving back home—five hours. It was a pretty quiet ride. I've not talked about it with my sisters, but I think that we were all deep in thought. Once we got back, I jumped in my car and headed to my apartment.

Day 7.

The day got off to a slow start. I opened the windows to allow the sunlight and a tiny breeze to pass through the apartment. I spent time doing a little more unpacking. Each box that I emptied somehow moved me. My thoughts, feelings, emotions—everything seemed to rise and fall like a roller coaster. At some point, I had to break the monotony. I decided to go for a ride. I had to get out. It felt like the walls were closing in on me.

I rode around for a bit without any specific direction. At times like this, I like to get out and be in nature. So, I decided to go to a park and go for a walk. When I pulled up to the park, I noticed a dog rescue shelter across the street. I decided to go to the shelter and look around; after all, I had absolutely nothing else to do.

When I entered the shelter, the lady working the desk took my information and then preceded to provide me with a tour of the facility. She showed me a ton of dogs. Finally, we came to a window with one little dog in it. The little dog was at the back-right corner of the viewing quad. On the glass in front of me was a sign that read, "I have 24 hours before I will be put down." This little dog was on death row. Even in such dire straits, this little fella sat up tall and looked me square in the eyes. He gave me a relentless stare. It was as though he was challenging me to speak. I asked the attendant to let me visit with him. She took me to one of the visiting pods where I sat and waited for her to bring him in.

She brought the little dog into the room. He walked all the way around the perimeter of the room a few times. Finally, he sat across from me and stared me in the eyes just like he had done when I was looking at him through the viewing window. Our conversation began, "Well, little buddy, you look like you've been through some things." I noticed that his ears were sore and that he had scratches on his face and welts along one of his sides. "What happened to you? Have you been fighting? Were you attacked? What's your story?" He did not respond at all—just the blank continuous stare. I said to him,

"I did not come here to get a dog—I don't have anything to offer you. My life is a hellhole right now. If you go home with me, I have to warn you, there isn't much there. It'll just be the two of us figuring things out. Are you sure that this is something that you want to be a part of?"

We sat in silence for a bit—at least three minutes or so of total silence. Finally, he stood up and walked over to me. He put his two front paws on my right knee and started sniffing me. I looked at him and sat still. He jumped up on the seat beside me and placed his head across my knee. I called the lady to take him back to the viewing quad.

After she put him away, I started asking her questions—how much? Has he had his shots? What are his needs? Does he have any medical issues? She said that he was good—no health issues. He'd had all of his shots. She said that if I would take him home, she'd insert the microchip for free and waive the adoption fee. Basically, every reason that I came up with to not adopt him, she found a way to work around it. She even gave me a collar, a leash, both water and feeding bowls, and a fifty-pound bag of dog food. So, I left with a dog named Chip.

We got back to the apartment as nightfall was setting in. We lay together in silence. My little buddy that I rescued off "death row" and I were on the air mattress, chillin. I looked at my watch. It was after midnight. Then, it happened. In all the silence, in all the reflection, in all the stillness—I had finally gotten it. We had found our Jerusalem, our place of peace. In an instant, it was revealed to me. The Divine Whisper spoke in the silence, "It is well. You guys will be just fine. You are aligned. You are ready to be transformed. It is time." The Seven Days of Hell were finally over.

Things started changing for me that night. As I lay on the mattress, I realized at that moment, my life was truly in alignment. I wasn't pressing to make anything happen. I wasn't holding on to the past. I was in a free space—available to and for whatever presented. I realized that in this space—a space of complete openness—all was available to me. I had begun being transformed. The Seven Days of Hell were finally over.

Let your light so shine before men, that they may see your good works, and glorify your Father which is in heaven.
                                                              —Matthew 5:16

The term "let" is an action verb suggesting that the human allows; in other words, we choose, and we choose using the God-given gift of reasoning. "Your light" means the God from within—the comforter that was left for us to have the capacity to cope with the familiar existence that we call life. "So shine"—means to illuminate with a radiant glow. This existence shall be observed by others that are your equal, thus "before men." In this case, the word "that" implies that there is a cause-and-effect relationship. "They" suggests that there is more than one—plural meaning, perhaps several. The word "may" means that there is an option available or that there is a lack of certainty. The ability to see, which is another action verb, means the opening of one's eyes. More importantly, it indicates the opening of one's mind such that the observer assigns meaning or creates a meaning for that which they observe or that of which they become aware. The phrase "of your" is assigned as a case of possession or ownership. The term "good" is descriptive of things considered positive. "Works" means the collective body of intentional efforts that have compensatory returns on efforts invested. The word "and" connects the first portion with the second portion, meaning they are not mutually exclusive, but are in fact inherently connected. The phrase "to glorify" denotes to intentionally bring public and collective honor to "your Father," the person and possessive giver or creator of life. The designation of a specific location, in other words—"which is." Finally, "in heaven" that is a space in the presence of God, the source of all that is good.

In short, transformation is a working process that may be observed and celebrated by others with the knowledge that the visible changes are a result of communing with a power greater than the human. I call this source God. There are so many names, and people can really get stuck in the space of the "right" name. That is not at all relevant. The point is that when we speak spirit to spirit, it is a Divine experience. In truth, the mystery of these moments is beyond our normal comprehension. It is the universal bond that connects us. It is the essence of abundant life. More accurately stated, it is a cosmically binding unique experience. It is something that you and I feel.

Chip and I lay on the air mattress; all of a sudden, life looked different. Remember the sunglasses? It was like putting on my new sunglasses. Everything had a new, clear freshness. Alignment leads all of us to a sign of greater courage and unshakable confidence. It provides a different dance partner for life's journey. Staying in alignment is done by simply staying available and listening for the Divine Whisper. It is from this space that Truth is revealed. It is from this space that understanding begins to grow inside each of us. If each person who is a part of the human race could simply stay in alignment, how different would the world be?

Pain and pondering are tied to the past. Power is connected to the present. Prosperity is grounded in the promises of God or whatever you choose to call that which is greater than yourself. Since that night, I have been intentional about staying in alignment. It is a simpler life. On that night, I became me. I am not strange nor are you. Wherever you are, wherever you're stuck, or maybe you're not stuck at all. Maybe you're on top of the world right now; it doesn't matter—your destiny is calling for you.

Reflection Questions:

1. Who are you?
2. Are you in alignment with that which is greater than yourself?
3. What are the things that are pulling you out of alignment?
4. What are the things that are pulling you into alignment?
5. What intentional efforts are necessary for you to pull yourself into alignment?

_____

_____

_____

_____

_____

_____

_____

_____

_____

_____

_____

_____

_____

_____

_____

_____

_____

_____

_____

_____

_____

_____

_____

_____

_____

_____

_____

_____

_____

_____

_____

_____

_____

_____

_____

_____

_____

CHAPTER 2

A SEVERED AND SEVERELY
SEARED CONSCIENCE

Man has studied the process of procreation from time immemorial. With the continuing advancements in technology and science, we are still dependent on God for the formation of life. This is yet to be explained. There are factors that may influence or increase the possibility of conception and the probability of a sustainable life; however, there is not a documented demonstration where the human had the final say, or the sovereign capacity to make the final decision to actually give life. We can only measure probability. Successful procreation is an act of God.

For the human, the father plays a vital role in the process of insemination. The fetus is intimately connected to the mother as they bond during the pregnancy. This timeframe is divided into three trimesters totaling nine months. During this period, the inherent connection between the mother and the embryo is, in fact, literal. For example, whatever the mother eats, for all intents and purposes, the developing baby eats. Whatever the mother drinks, the baby drinks. With these things being said, most people would agree that this basic demonstration of both physiological and behavioral patterns is observable.

Deductive reasoning would suggest that life begins with a direct connection to God. If we accept it or not, from that moment, we—human beings—spend the rest of our lives trying to reconnect with God. This is a confounding factor for the "severed and severely seared conscience." So then, what does it mean to have a "severed and severely seared conscience"? This perception of the perpetual disconnection from the original source of life, though only in perception, is where the severing takes place. It is fairly easy to see that we, human beings, lose that direct pipeline to the source of all and become inherently connected to similar beings, specifically mother and father, and the rest of the chromosomal linkages that shape our genetic composition. Thus, it may be surmised that this is the origin of the cutting or severing of the human from the giver of life. The divine umbilical cord has the appearance of having been severed. It is hard to really grasp the depth of what has been romanticized into a mere snipping of the cord. Let me show you what I mean.

I was fortunate to have the opportunity to play college football. I was not the biggest guy, but I was relatively fast. I played wide receiver. I ran well-disciplined routes and I could catch a BB in the dark while wearing a blindfold and metal gloves. If I could touch the football, I caught it.

We were in the second quarter of one of our games. It was fourth down and the ball was on the opponents' thirty-three-yard line. My coach yelled, "Punt return! Punt return!" I heading out from the sideline onto the field. I was the returner—the deep guy. My job had three parts—first, make sure that there were eleven of us on the field; second, catch the football; and third, get to the wall and run.

I stood back readying myself to receive the punt. I counted to be certain that there were ten of my teammates in front of me. I looked to the sideline for the special team's coach to call the play for the return. The signal was for "return right." This meant that the blocking scheme would be set for me to catch the ball and, of course, head in the direction of the right sideline as soon as I saw a crease. If I could just get to the hash, I'd have a wall of blockers to escort me to the end zone. I relayed the call to the rest of the return team and steadied myself.

"Hut!" came from behind the opponent's line. The ball was snapped back to the punter. Less than a second later, the punter launched a walloping kick. It was a high and tight spiral. I watched the ball turning and spinning. I tracked it like a Patriot missile as it reached its peak height before turning and heading toward the earth like a heat-seeking destroyer that I was tasked with catching. In a split second, I had to determine whether there would be an opportunity to safely secure the ball and attempt to get to the wall. I saw my lead blocker peal out and circle to ensure my safe reception of the ball. I saw the opponents' relentless pursuit. They forged in my direction faster than usual. It seems as though they had jumped the start because they closed on me so quickly. I had to decide.

My right hand went up high into the air, signaling for a fair catch. This meant that I was not to be touched and that I was to be provided with space to catch the football. As I settled under the missile, and prepared my hands and body for the jolt of the leather missile speeding toward me, it happened. There was an explosion! And then, silence …

The next sound was that of a high-pitched piercing bell. It was like the flatline sound that an electrocardiogram machine—a heart monitor—makes when life is no more. I paused. The stillness of movement lay gently against the backdrop of the steady high pitched bell. I had been hit. The ball never reached me. One of the destroyers from the opposing team hit me before the ball arrived. He had a full head of steam and ran right through me like an eighteen wheeler running through an intersection and t-boning a compact car that was sitting in the middle of the intersection. The top of his helmet crashed through my chin. My head was back because I was looking up at the ball preparing to make the catch. Upon contact, my entire body snapped back and exploded against the ground as the collision was like a fatal car crash. And then the flatline, the nothingness of stillness. The silence and the shock of that which cannot be explained. The devastation and trauma separating all that is natural. At that moment, it was like trying to understand a new existence. Everything was familiar, but nothing was the same.

This is what it is like when the cord of life, as we know it, is severed. Though we lack the capacity to fully grasp what happens when it happens, this is emblematic of the shock of having the umbilical cord severed. As life starts happening, the very tips of the cord that was once the lifeline for our existence are slowly and tediously seared—burned by the pain and trauma of everyday life. Each day, we move a tiny bit further away from the origin until we are awakened. Some never experience the awakening. They exist in this foreign slumber until they depart this life and return to the source from whence they've come.

The human being continues to evolve until the day of stillness occurs. Total stillness is not achieved until death knocks and beckons for us to be moved from this life. So then, one can only ponder the process. When we accept this process and embrace that which is new, we move to a space of truth. And it is from that truth that each individual's calling is fulfilled. It is in that truth that we respond to the whisper that touches our core of existence and shapes our marrow to be who we are called to be.

When we are born, each of us is born into a unique set of circumstances that are not of our own selection. We have a destined inheritance based on the simple composition of our genetic base. The fabric of our DNA most certainly affects how our path will begin to unfold. We do not get to choose the color of our eyes, the texture of our hair, and the color of our skin. We do not get to choose if our family is wealthy or poor, or if we are naturally an introvert or an extrovert. We do not get to select our culture and heritage. We simply have to go with the flow of our destined arrival.

At our birth, somebody becomes responsible for shaping our beliefs. In most cases, this duty falls on the parents. However, there are times when these tasks or opportunities to invest and pour into the lives of another person end up on the shoulders of the extended family. There are cases when the force of nature yields that someone, other than biological connections, has to fulfill the task of raising a child. Regardless of the "who," somehow the core set of beliefs for the human takes shape. This is an ever-evolving process. As we move through the path of growth, somehow the beliefs shift into what we call the individual's perception. Perception is the perspective through which we see the things that we encounter through direct contact or through vicarious exposure.

Over time, it is the combination of the situation and beliefs that stimulates the choices we make or our behavioral patterns. We make choices that are consistent with our aggregate at any given point in the journey of life. These choices demonstrate consistency over time; thus, the pattern takes shape.

Is it possible for the flow of personal circumstances to impact the perceptions of that which is true, and finally, the consistent ebb and flow of the choices that we make during our lifetime? Do the choices we make influence or impact our personal situation? I argue that this pattern is bidirectional for example, the pattern can flip and go in the opposite direction. Our behavioral choices may influence how we see things and ultimately impact what we believe to be true. With the shifting of our beliefs, sometimes our situation or unique set of circumstances experiences change. Of course, if the patterns continue in this direction, with the shifts in our situation, we may choose differently with our behavioral choices.

It is important to distinguish that this is not a discussion of physiology and anatomy. If we look at the variables previously mentioned through the lenses of a social scientist, the concepts are relatable in a different way. The concepts of social cybernetics are applicable. If we start with the idea of the triadic brain, clarity is revealed. (De Gregori, W. *Social Cybernetics: An Interdisciplinary Approach to Social Sciences and Human Development.* Chicago: Free University for Feedback of the Americas, 1980.)

The triadic brain is a concept that suggests that the brain and its functions may be divided into three subsectors. This contributes to the behavioral choices that people make on a consistent basis. It is proposed that the left-brain serves as the center for linear thinking. It is the portion of the brain that facilitates the coordination and storage of facts that drive our decisions. It also proposes that the right brain serves as the creative center, the spiritual hub, the space that supports what we feel. The central brain nourishes the element of survival. It is proposed that this portion of the triadic brain gives insight on the relationship between cause and effect. These three concepts together form what are the constructs for the three-part brain, the triadic brain.

When we begin to categorize and associate the choices that we make on a daily basis, these minimal concepts begin to reveal, at the least, a basis for transformation. We, as human beings, begin to become more aware of our behaviors. Raised awareness of our behaviors is the starting point of transformation. The "severely seared conscience" comes from the many pains and discomforts of life. How, then, does one nourish this ever-evolving process of change? The answer is simple. We have to make a decision. We have to decide if we will wake up or continue in the slumber that is a death march. For so many, day after day, they choose to continue to slumber through choosing to remain in a state of the severely seared conscience.

That day, on the football field, I made a decision. I got up.

After the collision, for a second, I lay on the ground determining if I had the capacity to get up. My engrained grit and sheer will would not let me stay down. I rolled over and pushed myself up to my feet. I knew in an instant that there were some things that were not right. But I got up.

A few hours later, I was in surgery where a few things had to be addressed. One of my teeth would have to be replaced. My chin and the left side of my jaw was broken. The jaw bone on the left side of my face had pierced the outer canal of my ear. A metal plate with screws was placed in my chin to hold it together. The left side of my jaw was reset and my mouth was wired shut. The outer ear canal was left to heal on its own. The doctor told me that had I been hit one centimeter lower, he was certain that I would have been paralyzed from my neck down. The impact of the blow would have severed my spine, breaking my neck and destroying the nerves running through my spinal cord.

Roughly twelve weeks later and several vanilla milkshakes that I could slurp through the whole from my missing tooth, I was back on the field feeling better than ever and was back catching punts.

The recovery and healing all started with me making a decision. That day when I got hit, everything about me went numb in that split second. Up to that point, I had prided myself on being a tough guy, a true football player. That day—on that one play, in that very moment—I faced a pivotal point. We all have those moments. We all have specific times in our life when we can see where we stood at a crossroad and was faced with a decision that could change the trajectory of everything. On that day and in that moment, I made a decision.

I got up.

Reflection Questions:
1. List out the facts that are your "situation."
2. Make a list of your perceptions.
3. Make a list of behavioral patterns that have worked well for you.
4. Make a list of behavioral patterns that have occurred but have not truly served your greater good.
5. What are you willing to do differently?
6. What must you do differently?

_____

_____

_____

_____

_____

_____

_____

_____

_____

_____

_____

_____

_____

_____

_____

CHAPTER 3

IN THE DIRECTION OF HEALING

Moving from a severed and severely seared conscience to a space conducive to healing is a process. It begins in the disarming of the defensive shell that has subconsciously been put in place as a result of pain. Fear is at the foundational construct of previously experienced pain that now acts as a force field rooted in events over time. The act of disarming sets the stage for transformation.

The starting point or points of connection that shape the defensive posturing have to be identified so that a road map to healing and wholeness may be assembled. Disarming is about bringing clarity to the sources of the various points of pain, after which confounding factors may be disassembled and the seeds of prolific visioning, of returning to that which was lost in what has already been described as "a severed and severely seared conscience." The disarming is a mining process that separates the morsels of truth from the painful illusions that really create limiting beliefs.

The reality is that people already know the truth. They just need a little help accessing it. And that help looks a bit different for every individual. This is the willing nurturing of a safe and sacred space within the person where the fluid exploration of connecting to the source of all, God, provides the rewriting of a person's DNA. The chromosomal elements are rewired in a way that allows a fresh and invigorating perspective to be established, thus reshaping the person's view of life and the possibilities for the remaining life journey that awaits their response to the divine beckoning for their specific existence. It's about going back to the place of pain, the place of hurt, in order to create the opportunity for forgiveness of others and more impactful, the forgiveness of oneself. This is an internal dialogue that removes the chances of rationalizing the illusions and the birthing of the truth—the destined truth. When we hold on to pain, we inherently change the trajectory of the path to our destiny. We irrevocably alter our path to peace. Transformation is about accepting what is the truth and moving away from what are illusions and falsities into the zeal of liberty.

Remember that truth has the capacity to withstand the rigors of time. The accessing of this information and the shaping of it into a completely different path for going forward is an awakening of what was destined at conception, prior to the severing of the conscience. The formation of a seal that bonds the sorrows of life's painful times allows the defensive shell to be broken and left behind. The broken pieces are used for the birthing of a peaceful, more fulfilling existence. This life is the new normal. It is life, and life more abundant. The natural question is, how does one experience the "disarming"?

One Saturday morning, I was sitting in the living room of my home, relaxing and watching TV. The phone rang, and it was one of my longtime clients, Monte. As soon as I answered, he started talking like a burst of energy saying, "I have something to share with you that is going to blow your mind." I was a bit of confused, wondering what did he have to share? He was so excited. He said, "I had a dream last night. I know exactly what you are supposed to do." I was still confused, so I sat quietly and waited for her to say more. "Last night I dreamt that there was a boxing match and I was one of the fighters. I never saw the face of the opponent, but you were there, Dr. J! You were right there in my corner. That is it! You were right there, in the corner! You were my cornerman." I thought, "What?"

"You were there. You are there for me like you are there for so many people. You are a cornerman. I was in a fight for my life, and there you were guiding me. Leading me into my strategy. You are a cornerman! You help people navigate through their fights!"

I must admit that I was completely confused when he started talking, but in the next few minutes, it was revealed that he was right. I am a cornerman.

We have all experienced watching the ultimate pugilistic sport, boxing. There's nothing like it. The energy in the air. The anticipation of two athletes in top shape, completely prepared—ready for battle. Boxers are modern-day warriors. In today's world, big fights are televised or live streamed to most parts of the world. While watching on pay per view or live stream, fight fans can only try to contain their excitement. Boxing is violent, but everybody loves a good fight!

The fighters descend from the quiet of the pre-fight dressing room with an entourage. They make their way to the ring. Sometimes it is hard to know if they are getting hyped for the fight or if they are trying to calm their nerves. Typically, the contender is the first to make their way to the ring. With much fanfare and hoopla, the rhythm of the entire arena begins the cheering for their chosen gladiator. The exuberance of the no-nonsense sporting event and one of the most primitive explosions of the reptilian brain bubble up to the surface with uncontrollable excitement.

When the champion exits the dressing room, the arena erupts. Nowadays, there is usually a camera that tracks the fighter from the door of the dressing room, down long winding corridors and hallways in route to the platform that is to be the showcase for the evening. By the time the champion climbs the steps and dips under the ropes entering the ring, the place is ready to explode. So much of the experience is about this brief period of time—the moments of anticipation right before the fight actually starts.

Even non-boxing fans have seen this unfold. We are all drawn into the allure and magnitude of the moment. Of an even greater magnitude are the challenges of this life's journey. And here's the thing: most of the time, we don't have witnesses when we're in the fight of our lives.

The commentator calls for the attention of the entire arena while the gladiators prance about, showcasing their preparedness for the battle that is about to begin. The commentator announces the "tale of the tape." This is when the crowd hears the official comparison of the fighters. Their win-loss records are revealed. Their unique personalities are frequently a calculated brand reflecting their customized style of engagement, such as hitman or bone crusher … etc. This is all a part of the show. Finally, their names are called out in a spectacular way. This all adds to the sheer excitement of the moment. As spectators cheer and jeer, they—the fighters—are the epitome of showmanship and focus as the referee calls the fighters to the center of the ring. The basic rules and expectations are stated. The fighters touch gloves, return to their corners, and make final preparations for the opening bell. Finally, all supporters, promoters, hype extras, and the cornermen are asked to leave the ring. Then it happens. The bell rings! The fighters meet at the center of the ring, touch gloves, and begin the process of implementing the game plan that they have studied, adjusted, and practiced for months in preparation for this very moment.

Each boxer listens ever so intently to what the opponent reveals through the "feeling out process." This is a careful back-and-forth shuffle. Touch here. Touch there—the leather meets the skin of the opponent. Unless one of the competitors clearly outmatches the other, this round is about checking out the opponent. It is about checking to see if there's validity to what they've studied and thought to be true of the opponent from the countless hours of training camp. This is the chant of the first round. The bell rings, and both fighters return to their corners.

There is usually at least one or two other persons in the corner beside the actual cornerman. Their job is to manage the condition of the fighter as the fight unfolds. They provide the fighter with a shot of water, rinse off the mouthpiece, do a quick massage to the upper torso that is the tattered and worn body of the fighter, and wipe down visible bumps and bruises. They wipe the face down with grease so that the surface is less likely to tear when the leather of the gloves pinches and spins the flesh upon contact. Everybody in the corner is very aware of their role and is fully committed to working together to tend to the gladiator as the battle evolves. Nonetheless, there is not a discussion about who is in charge of the operations of the corner. The designated space for revisiting the fight plan is the space of the cornerman. The cornerman is the dominant voice in the corner between rounds for the duration of the fight.

By fight night, the cornerman and the boxer have spent countless hours studying the opponent—picking away at their strengths and planning strategies to exploit their weaknesses. This duo shapes a game plan for the fight and diligently trains to prepare for executing the plan on fight night. The cornerman has the ultimate role of piloting the fighter on fight night. This means constantly checking in with the fighter to assess their capacity to perform at their highest possible level at any given moment over the course of the fight. They have to see things that the fighter cannot see for themselves. They have to, at times, serve as the voice of reason because the fighter is so vested in the pursuit of victory that they will literally fight themselves to death.

The dialogue between the fighter and the cornerman during the fight is a mixture of science and art. The cornerman is the scientist with a proven formula that has been tested. The fighter is the artist that shapes the beauty of a "one-of-a-kind" piece that is destined to be hung in the spotlight of integrity for all to admire. Some may like the design. Others may not appreciate the creativity of the craftsman, but all shall admire the quality of the work.

This is where the copilot checks to see that all measures are accurate and reminds the gladiator of the game plan. The fighter listens and prepares for the next round. As the fight rolls forward, the team of comrades works synchronously to adjust the plan—the strategies. As the fight dictates both the rhythm and the dance, modifications to the prefight game plan have to be adjusted.

For the casual fan, the relevance of the strategy may be difficult to see. The more seasoned fight fans are able to see the plot with its many twists and turns as the gods of pugilism display their talents and shortcomings. The fighters are actually in the ring, exchanging blows, slipping, and sliding punches—bob and weave! Bob and weave. Jab! Jab! Slip! The action is relentless and calculated. All that is the technical chivalry of the fight is celebrated or shunned by the clear and biased fans. Nobody is really clear and informed, but all are passionate from their own perspective.

One Saturday night, my brother and I were watching a championship fight on pay per view. One of the fighters in the ring was actually one of the kids that I knew and encountered when I coached little league football. The fighter, who shall remain nameless, was defending his crown as world champion in his weight division. I was so excited to see him fight. So many of the guys from the little league had told me how good he was, but I had not had a chance to see him fight. Well, this particular night was the night to see him doing his thing. To my surprise, it was his opponent and his opponent's cornerman that really stole the show, at least for me. Right before my eyes, on one of the biggest stages that a professional fighter can hope to experience, the fighter and his corner man spoke "spirit to spirit."

The champion that I had known since he was a kid was clearly dominating, pretty much the entire fight. What was interesting is that the opponent's cornerman had known both of the fighters since they were kids. In fact, there was a time when both of them actually trained out of the same gym. They had even been sparring partners years ago. Anyway, this guy was clearly getting dominated in the fight. The cornerman was actually also his father. The camera crew followed him to his corner between the ninth and tenth rounds.

The cornerman said, "Son, you are going to have to show me something or I'm going to call it! I'm worried about you. You don't look like yourself. Do you want me to call it?"

The fighter said,

"You're my cornerman. Do your job! I trust you! I'm a fighter! ... I am here to fight! If you say that it's over, then it's over!... I'm going to fight until the fight is over! ... You have to make the call! I'm a fighter! I'm gonna keep fighting!"

This guy's left eye was swollen almost shut. It was so apparent that he was being outmatched in every aspect of the fight, except one area—that was having and demonstrating the heart of a champion. He was not going to quit. My brother and I both watched without saying a word. Something different was happening at that moment. We have watched a bunch of fights together. We both knew that there was something special happening between the fighter and his cornerman. In all of the fights that we've watched together, neither of us had ever seen anything like this.

The look on the face of the cornerman was one of concern and uncertainty. It was so obvious that there was a battle going on inside of him. Should he allow his fighter to continue? Should he allow his son to continue to be destroyed by, on this particular night, a flat-out better fighter? The cornerman/father looked at his fighter and looked across the ring at the champ. The cornerman's face was tense. There was hesitancy in his voice. There was uncertainty in his eyes ... There was an awkward silence.

The bell rang to start the tenth round. As the fighters began to move toward each other, the cornerman threw in the towel. And just like that, the fight was over.

My brother and I looked at each other, and neither of us said a word. It was a moment that simply made sense to us both. I knew that he was not thinking about the fight that we'd just watched, nor was I. As the fighters met up in the center of the ring after the fight, the champ congratulated his opponent and longtime friend for the valiant effort in the fight. The contender congratulated the champ. When the contender's cornerman hugged the champ and congratulated him, he said to the champ, "I had to stop it. You know how he is. He didn't really want me to stop it, but I had to. I couldn't let my son truly get hurt. You're on your way to being one of the greatest boxers of all time. Great fight tonight. I'm proud of you."

If when in the battles of life, we could all experience the intense focus and spectacle that is the ultimate competition—mano a mano. This is not the platform for everyday gladiators. We are all in training, if you know it or not. Day after day, we prepare for the engagements that shape the course of each person's unique journey. The levels of the opponent will vary from moment to moment—from situation to situation. We each have the things that set us apart from the next person. But one thing is certain. We all have to fight.

When facing the opponents that present the true test of who we are as individuals, we have to be able to see the opponent as they make their way to the ring. One has to train—and train daily just like the warriors of old and the gladiators of today. The process of preparing for the fight is about the fighter investing every ounce of energy, every single drip-drop of sweat, blood, and tears, every molecule of fortitude, and every granule of sheer unadulterated courage into the preparation process. Each individual must train for the fight—the fight that is life. This opponent plays for keeps. Every individual must approach these battles like a hungry and relentless contender who is determined to defeat the champion and leave the ring and the arena bearing the spoils of victory. And to the defeated falls the enigma of immortality. The contender has to be tenacious in order to take the title from the champion. The contender has to truly beat the champion.

Sometimes it is incredibly difficult to even know that you are in a fight. This level or degree of vulnerability is subconsciously a by-product of the severed and severely seared conscience. This is the numbness that allows the opponent to lull each of us into a foreign space of battle. Sometimes, we are so deeply submerged in the fight for our life that there is an inordinate amount of recovery needed to have a small chance at victory. This is the space where the cornerman earns the wages of a master tradesman. The cornerman has to help the fighter to disarm and disassemble the opponent.

In order to disarm the opponent, the contender has to first gain a clear and accurate knowledge of their own gifts and talents. It is easy to assess these tools on the physical plane. If you walk into a boxing gym, a seasoned trainer—a good cornerman—can watch you move for two minutes and tell you what your physical attributes are and what you need to do to polish your skills to perform at a significantly higher level. You must know what your tools are and develop them—hone them to ensure that you maximize every piece of what makes you a gifted foe. The bottom line here is that there is not a substitute for doing the work. You must do the work to be better. To be your best—you must do the work.

Now, let's be clear. It is much more complex to assess the deeper, more incessantly valuable, and consistent beat that is the heart of a fighter. There is not a simple way to identify the capacity of a fighter's heart, as this is naturally the most steady and consistent part of the human's composition. Just because a person has a heart that beats steadily does not mean that he is a real fighter. What makes a real fighter is the sheer, simple, and raw true grit—the toughness to keep punching and moving forward—no matter what. In a boxing gym, the only way to assess this is to put on the protective gear, shove a mouthpiece past the lips, cinch up the gloves, ring the bell, and fight. It will not take long to find out if you have "it" or not. The "it" is the heart of a fighter—the brutal toughness to withstand getting hit, possibly even being knocked to the canvas. The ultimate measure in the gym is, will an individual get up, regroup, and keep punching?

To disarm the opponent that is life, we all must know what our unique gifts are. We must find the heart and tenacity to fight back. We have to prepare like a wise and crafty champion who has been in many competitive battles. Great champions, most of the time, find a "way out" to outwit, to outperform, to win on the big stage—retain the championship title, as every great champion has done.

All of the hours of training … culminates in this, the final round. This is it. In the next three minutes, all that has been done so far in the fight must conclude. Who will take the final round and remove all questions from the onlookers, and most importantly, the three judges at ringside? How might the battles of the modern-day gladiators match up with the epic triumphs of the warriors of yesteryear? In sporting events like boxing, there are external factors that influence the outcome. However, in the game of life, each individual must assess themselves. What will determine victory, for each of them, as life goes forward? Each of us gets the opportunity to choose.

The process of disarming and moving in the direction of healing is not about the opponent, but it is about disarming oneself. In the game of life, in order to initiate and execute the disarming process, there are some basic things that each of us has to do. Each person has to fully acknowledge that there is pain or fear. It is extremely helpful to identify the origins of pain or fear. Each person has to find a way to forgive others who contributed to the pain equation. More importantly, each person has to find a way to forgive oneself. Forgiveness offers a person the elusive freedom that is hidden by the illusion of pain.

Just as the great warriors of old and the modern gladiators, it is helpful to have a cornerman. That person may play a key role in the disarming process that allows us to move in the direction of healing. A great deal of the work is of an internal nature. Needless to say, it is helpful to have a witness—a second set of eyes—to help you to see the things that you may not be able to see for yourself.

When in the throes of the many battles of life, like a boxer, we all have a certain level of natural talent. It is helpful to have the right person to bear witness and to provide the stimuli that will help you stick to the game plan or to modify the game plan as the fight unfolds. This job is not one to be taken lightly; therefore, how does one know when they have identified the right cornerman? Well, the right cornerman is a lot like truth. The right person to bear witness demonstrates the ability to endure the rigors of life with you. They are there in the fight with you, but their point of view, at times, maybe a bit clearer than yours. The cornerman has to care enough about you to tell you the truth and to be free of judgment. They have to demonstrate the ability, over time, to speak truth to you from a place of love.

An individual's choice to disarm comes from a deep desire to move forward with their life—choosing to live into their destiny. Behavioral choices begin with a thought. The thought matures into a desire. The desire produces the options for action. Finally, the human makes a decision. This process repeats itself multiple times in a single day, a single hour, and even a single minute. Becoming aware of the power of this repetitive pattern means that it is not an automated cycle but instead becomes an engaging awareness that integrates the head, the heart, and the hands and feet. This results in the residual effect of intentional calmness or perhaps a greater sense of awareness. Regardless of the preferred terminology—and there are many options—the bottom line is that this results in a greater sense of alignment with those things that are true.

So what happens when you don't have the cornerman as I mentioned earlier—the guy who was both a father and a cornerman? Not everybody is fortunate to have such compassionate and caring people in their lives. I've read books and thought to myself that I didn't have any of the things that were described in the books. I have been fortunate enough to have conversations with people who have been and truly are world changers. I have walked away from some of those conversations feeling like, "What about me? I don't have all of those things? I don't have a butt load of money nor a cornerman. So, what am I supposed to do?" I have discovered that we really do have all that we need. We have to simply learn how to gain access.

Monte was right. It is helpful to have a good cornerman. But sometimes, the reality is that with or without a cornerman, there is work that has to be done. For some of these things, an individual simply has to make the decision. They have chosen to be better. And being better is not always easy. Sometimes it requires us to search for the best that is within us.

How much time are you investing in yourself for the fight for your life? What are you doing with that time? What has been the return on that investment? What are you going to do to create habits that support your destiny?

The first thing is that you have to make a decision.

Reflection Questions:

1. List the items that you need to "disarm." What or who are you battling? Why is the fight underway? Where did the fight begin? Who and/or what do you have to forgive?

2. What are the "truths" that you know about each of these items?

3. Based on the "truths," what are your next three steps?

4. Do you have a cornerman? If so, how are they working out for you? What do you really need in a cornerman?

5. What engaging awareness has to occur to integrate the head, the heart, and the hands and feet?

6. In what way(s) are you more aligned with the truth?

_____

_____

_____

_____

_____

_____

_____

_____

_____

_____

_____

_____

CHAPTER 4

THE FOUR DISCIPLINES
OF INTENTION

Making the decision to live into your destiny is no whimsical, misleading self-talk exercise. It requires that you "make a decision." It requires each of us to "make a decision" to do the things that will propel us into our destiny. The universe listens to our requests at the biocellular level. It is from that space that the request of our desires is surrendered to God. What's on the request list?

Whatever you want.

How then do we submit the request such that the Master hears and responds to it?

Regardless of the faith journey, there are disciplines that are intended to strengthen the person—to position the individual to go deeper within, thus nurturing them internally to reach further externally. There are practices that cut across all denominations and faith communities. Most religious sects consider prayer, meditation, the study of sacred literature, and worship to be cornerstones of daily life. These disciplines create the space for spiritual experiences that result in clearer thinking, a deeper understanding of oneself, and, most importantly, a deeper understanding of that which is greater than the human—whatever or whoever that is for you.

The formula for creating successful disciplines is quite simple. If the human is able to be intentional about the experiences of prayer, meditation, the study of sacred content, and worship, there is a subtle transformation that occurs in that person's life.

Prayer is analyzed extensively in the literature. It is viewed by some as one-way communication. It is the space where the human speaks to God. It is the platform where people have the opportunity to pour out their deepest concerns, to proclaim their greatest joys, to release the echoes of pain, to celebrate success, to cry out for forgiveness, and to embrace the peace of a comforting heart. The focus of this time varies from individual to individual and from situation to situation. Frequently, the human prays for others and circumstances that appear to be far beyond his capacity to affect. Prayer provides the restoration of hope and the calm resolve of comfort for those who practice it with any degree of consistency. Needless to say, there is not a right or a wrong way to pray. The discipline is about talking directly to God in whatever way serves the person best.

Meditation is a time for reflection. It is a time for hearing God's voice. It is described differently by many groups. There are some who believe sitting, standing, or lying in a certain posture may position the human for a moment of enlightenment. Others believe that meditation can occur simultaneously while doing other things. An example of this may be the experience of riding in the silence of a car while commuting to work. This quiet time may be the perfect time for some people to listen to God's voice. Regardless of the approach, this discipline is about listening.

Depending on the faith community, there is much sacred content available for ongoing study. Of course for the Christian, there is the Bible. For the Muslim, the Koran. For the Taoist, there is the Tao Te Ching. The list of various religious groups and their sacred content may go on and on. These scriptures, stories, or poetic verses all serve as nourishment for the reader. They create depth and dimension to the fundamental beliefs of those professing connection with any of these bodies. They provide content that yields great collective study, discussion, and connection with others who share the same set of beliefs. In some cases, the literature provides guidance at pivotal points in people's lives. For others, the sacred content may be reread and restudied. As a person evolves, so does their perspective about the readings. They offer content for the shaping of rich debates with those that believe the same or sharing opportunities with those that believe differently. The study of sacred content is ultimately about reading and reflecting on literature that helps to shape the human's thought processes, thus shaping the individual's perspective on and perception of all things in life. It is the "pouring in" of information that causes an individual to gain a deeper understanding of what he believes.

Worship again—regardless of the faith journey—is about the expression of value and appreciation of God's grace and mercy. It may occur as an individual's private experience or the collective experience of many who share in and profess the same beliefs. This unique experience is vastly different for everyone. Some may be overjoyed, and the expression of worship looks like an outpouring of emotions. For others, it may be the simple solemn stare as the mind listens for the voice of God or gives thanks to God. Some express their praise and worship through singing and/or the playing of instruments. Praise and worship have limitless stylistic expression variances. In a community of faith, there is typically a message shared by a minister—too many varied titles to try and choose the proper title in this text. In a community of faith, having all of these different forms of expression shared while in the same environment is worship. Although there may be an intentionally designed order of worship, it is a free-form endeavor. Worship is a celebratory praise for the goodness and graciousness of the Source. There are no limits on what this experience may be.

All four of the aforementioned disciplines have the capacity to be impactful for the individual. The daily disciplines of prayer, meditation, studying sacred content, and worship—all serve as nutrients for those desiring to grow in spirit. It is the intentionality behind these disciplines that makes all the difference. So, what does it mean to be intentional?

It is the focusing of one's actions that makes the difference. Some say that God knows the desires of our hearts and the utterance that speaks to our spirit. The intention is what creates the greatest return on these consistent exercises as the Four Disciplines of Intention. What would happen if we did all four of these disciplines every day for seven minutes a day? That is twenty-eight minutes of intentional time spent with God in four different ways. The focusing of efforts and the point of concentration are what makes the disciplines richer and more fulfilling experiences. It is the fixation of the mind on the task that takes all four to a completely new and transformative state.

Why seven minutes per day for each discipline?

The combination of cultural, historical, religious, numerical, and psychological factors all contribute to the allure of the number 7. It was prominent in many ancient cultures. (Winch 2018). Most famous of all were the seven "wonders of the world," which comprised the entire bucket list of every world traveler (the Great Pyramid of Giza, the Hanging Gardens of Babylon, the Temple of Artemis at Ephesus, the Statue of Zeus at Olympia, the Mausoleum at Halicarnassus, the Colossus of Rhodes, and the Lighthouse of Alexandria). In the Old Testament, the world was created in six days and God rested on the seventh, creating the basis of the seven-day-week we use to this day. In the New Testament, the number 7 symbolizes the unity of the four corners of the earth with the Holy Trinity. The number 7 is also featured in the book of Revelation (seven churches, seven angels, seven seals, seven trumpets, and seven stars). The Koran speaks of seven heavens, and Muslim pilgrims walk around the Kaaba in Mecca (Islam's most sacred site) seven times. In Hinduism, there are seven higher worlds and seven underworlds, and in Buddhism, the newborn Buddha rises and takes seven steps. The mathematician Alex Bellos asked 44,000 people to name their favorite number, and more than 4,000 of them named the number 7, far more than any other number.

In 1956, George Miller of Harvard University wrote what is today considered one of the classic papers in psychology in which he demonstrated that most people can retain roughly seven items of information in their short-term memory compared to their long-term memory. That is why phone numbers in the United States and many other countries tend to have seven digits (area code notwithstanding)—as most people are likely to recall the most digits (although cell phones did away with the need to recall anyone's phone number, even our own). Because of our mental capacity favoring seven items, seven is also a good fit for our attention spans, as long as the information is presented in seven groups. (Winch 2018). With all of this having been said, seven minutes per day is recommended for each of the Four Disciplines of Intention.

The processes of doing the Disciplines daily are similar to the organic farmer that tills the soil before planting the crop. The soil is turned over and turned over to stimulate all facets of its composition. This ensures that the soil is fertile, malleable, and prepared to be the landing place of seeds sown. A seed has to simply land in fertile soil to take root and begin to grow. Any precipitation allows the seed to settle into the soil. The roots go deeper into the earth and the stem and branches are then poised to reach for the sun. They grow toward the light. This is exactly what the Four Disciplines of Intention do for the human seedlings of connection to and alignment with the Source.

As already mentioned, we can pray in many ways. Many times, we spend a great deal of time interceding for others. Frequently, we petition God for those who are dear to us and for those who we know are facing all sorts of challenges. Sickness and perhaps the grieving of loss may be the focus of the conversation. Some have been made to believe that praying for oneself is selfish. I have found that to be to the contrary. In our society, selfishness has a bit of a negative connotation. I would offer that this prayer practice is rather specific and intimate. This speaks to the level of specificity and to the closeness of this type of dialogue with the one that is greater than yourself. Prayer for oneself makes for a richer day-to-day existence. It makes the journey of life easier, more palatable, and fulfilling. The reality is that this prayer is specific to the person offering prayer. It is really acceptable and desired to pray for oneself in truth and sincerity.

It is in this focused direct communication with God that we make clear the desires of our hearts. When we speak directly to God about our very own needs, as we see them, and the desires of our heart, as we feel them, something amazing happens. The intention of offering up that which weighs us down to the God who sustains our lives results in the human's capacity to dwell in a different space—a freer space, a life more abundant, a heart that maximizes its duty to love, and a spirit that is free to see and accept that which is true. For it is in truth that we find peace. The Master Architect is truth.

I prefer to call the discipline of meditation intentional listening. The exercise of bringing stillness to the mind does not occur without focus and intent. The natural function of the human consciousness is that of movement. The mind, even at its most relaxed state, continues to run—process even when the state of consciousness is rest. As accentuated by the Taoist and Buddhist, the exercise of willfully placing the mind in a state of rest while being conscious allows for the creation of space that allows the Divine Whisper to be the focal point of the listening experience. The whisper of the universe is quiet and oftentimes very clear. It is the busyness of the brain that interferes with the natural internal auditory function called listening. The process of listening in this manner must be cultivated. The environment and contextual positioning are factors that improve the potential outcomes of the effort of listening. It does require effort to maximize the monistic sharing from God. In essence, the bottom line is that if people intentionally position themselves to hear from the Source, the probability of them doing so is greatly increased. Now, there are times that within this designated seven minutes, as suggested earlier, the listener does not hear anything. The discipline is still effective. The intentional discipline creates space to hear the Divine Whisper at a later time. The intentional effort makes all the difference.

When the human pours quality information into the storage center of the spirit-self, the manifestation of this investment is rich. It is beyond a measurable value. This is the intentional discipline of reading sacred content. As already described, sacred content comes in many formats. Whatever the sacred volume is, it simply does not serve an individual if they fail to read and study the information. Frequently, the previous intentional disciplines are not as effective because the individual has not put quality reference information into the storage center, which includes both the mind and the heart. It is critical that the content read goes beyond simply being read. Cross-referencing other sources for purposes of bringing greater clarity to the content is necessary. Reading a fairly small amount of text with tremendous focus and self-reflection or internal rhetoric describes how this discipline is meant to function. This discipline of intention is not about the amount, but it is about the quality of consistent practice. To state emphatically, if high-quality, rich content is what goes in, high-quality, rich content is what will be processed. One must read enriching information to broaden the capacity to grow in depth and dimension spiritually.

Finally, the fourth Discipline of Intention is the matter of worship. Many people have very limiting beliefs about the subject of worship. There is certainly a value to the experience of corporate worship. It is well validated that the communal nature of corporate worship yields both inspiring and functional outcomes. The elements of tradition play a key role in managing the expectations of worship. Some would propose that when people are somewhat aware of what to expect, they are better equipped to get the max out of the experience. Others may argue quite the opposite, suggesting that giving space to the Holy Spirit to intervene and direct is more important. These matters of belief are certainly of merit and are considered by most communities of faith. Nonetheless, for many, worship is encapsulated as something that is done in an organized way, once or twice a week. The intentional discipline of personal worship is about increasing both the frequency and the autonomous needs of the individual. This concept may be more clearly defined as daily physical worship.

This discipline is a means of personally focusing on looking for God in daily life and celebrating God when God is seen. This may include the simplest of things like the smell of a freshly cut lawn, the chirping of birds early in the morning, the gentle caress of the wind on a fall afternoon, or perhaps the brisk direct cleansing offered by a spring shower. These examples are merely expressions of awareness and gratefulness to God. This discipline challenges the individual to go deeper.

Intentional physical worship is grounded in movement. On the physiological and anatomical levels, movement is the starting point for so many things that happen with the individual on a daily basis. The lack of physical movement becomes an inhibitor for worship. Now, it is accurate to say that people's individuality, physically, creates different levels of options for physical movement. Again, it is the intent that breathes life into this discipline. If an individual chooses to go for a short seven-minute walk on a daily basis, the physical movement stimulates the entire human microuniverse. If during the walk the person focuses on being aware of every part of the body and what it does in function for a closer connection to the Universe or the growth of God's kingdom or a moment of enlightenment, the experience immediately becomes a different experience. The intention is the differentiating factor of exercise or worship. Walking is but one simple example. The range of options is totally up to the individual. It is the act of intentionally connecting physical movement with personal expressions to God for the blessings of movement—regardless of limitations.

In sum, the Four Disciplines of Intention—intentional prayer, intentional listening, intentional study of sacred content, and intentional physical worship—are daily investments in the nourishment of one's spiritual connection to God. Answering the "why" question by clearly stating the causal motivation for doing each of the disciplines helps to cultivate consistency and the formation of daily habits. Initially, it should be anticipated that, though all four of the disciplines are not overwhelmingly difficult in theory, they do suffer from many interruptive competitors. The antics of daily life makes it easy not to commit to the twenty-eight minutes per day. If an individual is not willing to identify four seven-minute windows of time to give to these disciplines, what then is of value to the person's desire to sustain a spirit-filled life? So then, what is the value of that which sustains them?

Reflection Questions:

1. What has to happen for you to do the Four Disciplines of Intention daily in the next seven days?

2. What were the challenges within each discipline on day 1?
   a. Which of the disciplines did you do today?
   b. What caused you not to do your disciplines if you did not do them?
   c. How will you correct this so that you get all four disciplines done tomorrow?
   d. What was revealed to you today?

3. What were the challenges within each discipline on day 2?
   a. Which of the disciplines did you do today?
   b. What caused you not to do your disciplines if you did not do them?
   c. How will you correct this so that you get all four disciplines done tomorrow?
   d. What was revealed to you today?

4. What were the challenges within each discipline on day 3?
   a. Which of the disciplines did you do today?
   b. What caused you not to do your disciplines if you did not do them?
   c. How will you correct this so that you get all four disciplines done tomorrow?
   d. What was revealed to you today?

5. What were the challenges within each discipline on day 4?
   a. Which of the disciplines did you do today?
   b. What caused you not to do your disciplines if you did not do them?

   c. How will you correct this so that you get all four disciplines done tomorrow?

   d. What was revealed to you today?

6. What were the challenges within each discipline on day 5?

   a. Which of the disciplines did you do today?

   b. What caused you not to do your disciplines if you did not do them?

   c. How will you correct this so that you get all four disciplines done tomorrow?

   d. What was revealed to you today?

7. What were the challenges within each discipline on day 6?

   a. Which of the disciplines did you do today?

   b. What caused you not to do your disciplines if you did not do them?

   c. How will you correct this so that you get all four disciplines done tomorrow?

   d. What was revealed to you today?

8. What were the challenges within each discipline on day 7?

   a. Which of the disciplines did you do today?

   b. What caused you not to do your disciplines if you did not do them?

   c. How will you correct this so that you get all four disciplines done tomorrow?

   d. What was revealed to you today?

_____

_____

_____

_____

_____

_____

_____

_____

_____

_____

_____

_____

_____

_____

_____

_____

_____

_____

_____

_____

_____

_____

References

Winch, Guy. "Seven Reasons We Are Captivated by the Number Seven: Why a Simple Number has Such Psychological and Visceral Appeal." *Psychology Today Online*, December 20, 2018. https://www.psychologytoday.com/us/blog/the-squeaky-wheel/201506/seven-reasons-we-are-captivated-the-number-seven.

CHAPTER 5

THE PARADOX OF PAIN

When embarking upon the path of transformation, most people experience pain or at least some level of discomfort. How do you handle pain?

Pain is a common thing, and no one escapes it. If one figures out how to deal with pain, it becomes a source of growth. Such trauma presents an opportunity to get better. The valor of victory cannot be experienced without the nemesis of painful defeat. If there is not a challenge, then we can neither fully understand nor appreciate winning. If there is no pain, then we can neither understand nor appreciate being pain-free.

As long as the human being has life, there will be pain on some level. It is a variable that lurks in the shadows within, rearing its ugly head at odd and (in some instances) the most inconvenient times. At its core, pain is some type of discomfort. If we reflect, we all have, do, and will experience pain. It seeps out through our pores and hair follicles. It runs systemically throughout a being as though it has its own inherent path for reaching and touching the deepest cracks and crevices of our bodies. It has a direct wiring to our memory bank in three areas—our physical body, our mind, and our heart.

On the physical level, we all have memories as children of something that was painful. This does not end with youth; in fact, the probability of pain increases as we get older. As a child, I was told, "When you get older, that pain is going to come back on you."

As a boy, I was quite typical. Always running, jumping, climbing, and challenging the limits of the obstacle of fear. I was always testing the edges of discomfort. Sometimes, I escaped without the true essence of pain. Sometimes, I did not. I remember falling off of my bicycle the very first day of summer vacation when I was eight years old. It put a huge concrete/asphalt burn on my shin. I am reminded of the blood, the bright shiny hue of the open skin burn—the exhausting tenderness of healing. It took almost the entire summer to heal. When I look at that scar today, I am reminded of that spill. I find myself shaking my head and laughing because when it happened, it was such a big deal. And now, it is but a faint memory.

Pain may have been a bump, bruise, or scratch that left an indelible mark on the outer frame. On the physical level of our being, pain is easy to describe. Our body is equipped with indicators that inform us when something that is uncomfortable happens. The body immediately goes into the survival mode. The natural antibodies that are a part of who we are kick in, and the body begins to ward off the threat that is creating the pain.

The physical-self has an innate nature to attack the pain and fight it at the source. Over time, there is a healing process for the physical-self. There is frequently some kind of mark left that allows us to remember the pain. The skin, for example, leaves a scar if it has been broken or worn in such a way. When we see the scar, though it may no longer hurt as it did at the time of the trauma, the scar serves as a visual and contextual reminder of what once happened. If we all search ourselves, we will see evidence of physical pain that was once present. Some people struggle daily with chronic physical pain. Although demonstrable in its own right, the simplistic nature of pain on the physical level pales in comparison to pain in the space of our emotions.

There is a ton of literature on the subject of emotional pain. I don't feel the need to spend a great deal of time further defining this subject. The more traditional writings speak in an exhaustive way about what emotional pain is and its effect. I prefer to speak on the nature and the behavior of emotional pain.

Emotional pain takes up residence in our mind. It pauses itself for an internal ongoing dialogue that fights constantly for the dominant position. It uses the tenderness of emotional damage from emotional pain to capture its prey by simply speaking within the mind of its victim. Its voice is cunning and presents itself as though it knows you better than you know yourself. How then do we address the emotional pain? Let's start by giving it a name.

I refer to the voice of emotional pain as the ego-self. The ego-self is an internal perception of how one is being perceived by others. From this lens, emotional pain uses the road map of a person's past to stymie all that is good. The great majority of what is created by the ego-self is an illusion. This is not to suggest that emotional pain is not real. Emotional pain is real, but the human has the capacity to capture it and place it in a place where it may be of service to the greater good for a more abundant existence.

We have the tools to begin to quiet the leading voice of the master of illusions. By simply naming it, we then have a starting point for taming the elusive dance partner. This is the space where the memory and the voice of the ego-self use the stored data to manipulate, steal, kill, and destroy. Similar to the physical-self, pain on this level descends into our central storage center to be used as tools to keep us away from all that is good. The ego-self has a voice that is often very hard to distinguish. It is forever competing with the Divine Whisper that is within us all. Finding a means of determining which voice is speaking when the internal dialogue takes place is not always easy. The ego-self does not create. It only uses what is made available to it in the storage center.

When the challenges of life present themselves, the ego-self is such a vulnerable target that frequently pain on this level is in motion and we are not aware of its movement. It manifests itself in many ways, but of greater importance is its long-term presence. We think that we have dealt with the pain, yet we realize again that not only have we not dealt with it, but it is still alive and functioning in a covert manner. It is lying in the shadow of opportunity seeking an outlet to control. In the ego-self, pain truly is without power. It only has access to what we give it the power to affect. The ego-self is capable of containing and controlling the pain, but frequently our lack of awareness cannot recognize it for what it truly is. By the time we realize that it is moving, we have already been suckered in. Being able to name it—the voice of the ego-self—over time, the human becomes more aware, and that awareness diminishes the impact of master of the illusionist.

Emotional pain at this level has a great ally. That ally is fear. The ability to remember is the catalyst that allows pain at this level to gain access to power. When we remember the vivid discomfort of pain previously experienced, we begin to remove ourselves mentally because we do not want to hurt. The brain begins to direct us away from discomfort. This is the space where the ego-self choreographs the dance, courting the vulnerability of the human as it sorts through the blocking of memories stored in the tiny platforms of the human's memory. In search of clarity, the distinction is sought to determine the voice of the ego-self and the voice of the truth—the spirit-self. So, does this mean that the spirit-self experiences pain? No.

In the world of martial arts, many of the arts have a theory called "torque." To torque means to twist in an extreme and unusual manner. To move the body in a direction that it naturally turns, and then to twist it further, more extreme, the posture gains torque. This process is not comfortable; in fact, it creates a sense of discomfort, i.e., pain.

However, the reward of this uncomfortable positioning, though it seems to go against the natural order of things, actually not only challenges the natural order but elevates it. Once the body is in this extreme state of twist, there is pain. To further clarify this image, think of wringing out a wet towel.

If a person picks up a wet towel, holds it in both hands, and then takes both hands and turns them in opposite directions until the moisture from within the towel no longer drains out, then, turns the hands in the opposite direction even further, the towel drains out even the remaining droplets. Now, let's pause here.

Think about how the human body could turn in a similar manner such that the internal organs are momentarily drained and are twisted just a little bit further. This process produces an intense sense of discomfort—pain. However, the reward from this process is phenomenal. Unlike the towel, when released from this "torque" position, the human body unwinds, returning to its natural state. However, because of the recent twisting, the internal organs actually go through a bit of a cleansing and filtering process. As it returns to its natural state, new, freshly purified energy rushes through the internal organ and restores it to a refreshed and actually elevated state. If this intentional process of torquing of the human body is repeated frequently, great overall gains for the physical condition occur. What is the point?

The point is that, at times, we experience things that push us into a state of pain, but once we make the adjustment and deal with the impending issue, somehow, just like the internal organs, when we return to a more natural, less traumatic state, we are restored, replenished, and renewed. This is how the spirit-self deals with pain. It brings truth to that which is out of the ordinary. And because of that revelation, order is restored. We get better than we were before the exposure to the "pain." This is the effect and outlook of pain from the space of the spirit-self.

I am not exempt from the lure of emotional pain. There are but a few things more painful than the death of a loved one. I lost my mother, first to the onset of dementia, second to Alzheimer's, and finally to death. I believe that she transitioned from this life to an everlasting place of peace with God. Dementia crept into our lives like a thief moving in the dark, looking and lurking, seeking a point of entry. The robbery began with my mom having what appeared to be a seizure. She was rushed to the hospital and was placed in the intensive care unit. She had never had an incident like this before, so, we—my siblings and I—were all confused and frightened as the doctor began to explain.

The doctor shared that my mother was in a "stupor." To me, the stupor looked like a deep sleep, but she would have these sporadic verbal outbursts, as though she was having a really bad dream, and then she would return to this deep sleep. She was being fed through a tube, and monitors were all over her body. There were so many wires and cables. This visual image will be with me always. All of the vital signs that the clinical personnel typically monitor in the hospital were all within the normal ranges; however, she was not conscious. Of course, the doctors ran a multitude of tests. The results suggested that her brain was still firing properly, but her physical appearance and her lack of response were not consistent with the test results. Over the next few days, they began researching to further pin down a diagnosis. When I arrived at the ICU on day 3, I entered the room as the doctor was completing his rounds. I was completely smitten; when I walked into her room, the doctor was standing in the corner with this huge book on the table. He was writing notes about her levels, as indicated on the monitors. He was also looking in this huge book as a reference guide. The title of the book was *The Book of Autopsies*.

This "stupor" went on for sixteen days, and then just as quickly as it came, the stupor was gone—she simply woke up. We were all so very grateful, but things were never quite the same with my mother after the "stupor."

Mama returned to her home, to her normal living. She lived alone. She spent hours of her daily life talking on the phone with her church friends, reading God's word, and wrestling with the decisions and rewards of having lived a trying life. She loved discussing matters of the church and her relationship with the God Almighty, whom she loved so dearly. This was her escape from the escapades of everyday life. She was an elderly black lady with an eighth-grade education, who was once a strong black mama and somehow led a family. She had raised eight kids, who were now all adults and working professionally within their own chosen disciplines. We, her kids, were her pride and joy. She had a special and unique relationship with every one of us.

Over time, we started noticing things about Mama and the choices that she was making on a fairly consistent basis. She was different. First, it was Mama's driving. She was often confused and uncertain of where she was going. We started getting calls from my uncles, aunts, and a few of her friends. They all shared similar incidents of how my mother was lost and how they had to help her get back home or direct her to her destination. It wasn't long before we, her kids, had to put a stop to her driving. Next, it was the inability to do things around her house in a satisfactory manner; more importantly, she was no longer doing things in a safe manner. Her actions made us question her ability to live alone. Of course, even with the onset of dementia, it took some serious work on the part of us, her kids, to get her to give in—to get her to surrender her independence. We worked closely with her doctors. It was determined that the healthiest place for my mother was going to be in a nursing facility. We, her kids, searched for the right new home.

Life in this new setting was tough at first. It was tough on all of us. I remember going there alone to see her for the very first time. She greeted me with the same warmth and tenderness that I had known all of my life. She said, "Hey Baby! How are you doing? I am so glad to see you." I said to her, "Hey Mama. How are you doing? I'm so glad to see you."

I gave her a big hug and kissed her as I had always done. I asked, "Do you know who I am." She said, "Of course I know who you are. You are my baby brother." ... My heart sank. Words simply would not come out. I was speechless. It had come to this.

My mother—the woman who gave me life; the woman who was my first teacher; the woman who calibrated my moral compass; the woman who cleared the path and pointed me in the direction of God; the woman who was the rod of discipline and the staff of support; the woman who was my first love—she was gone. My mother did not know my name.

Words cannot capture the pain that I felt on that day. There was an emptiness like no other. For me, there has never been a shriller sound than the reverberation of my heart bouncing on the ceiling of hell to a point of stillness. My world literally stopped. The ground on which I stood became the embodiment of gravity. It felt as though the core of everything that I had ever known began to leave my body. All about me became dark. I felt heavy. My body began going into the survival mode—my heart, for a moment stopped beating. My physical-self felt like it was shutting down. There was a boulder in my throat and a tombstone that slipped through the resting place where my heart bellowed for comfort. My eyelids lost their function—they were not able to be the dam for the emotional outpouring of my pain. Tears ran from my face in search of a landing place, and just like my falling heart, they would not find a home. In that instance, the pain changed my life forever.

This was not the end of the journey. I watched as Mama gave in to the call of nature on her physical-self. She shrank before my eyes, and I shrank before the God who created us both. Eventually, she gave in to the plight and the limits of this, her earthly home. She transcended the parameters of human life. Alas, she was set free. She returned to the source that gave her life. And it is there that she sits in a house not made by hands.

Through the process of full-blown dementia, the gentle and confusing caress of Alzheimer's disease, and at last, the triumphant march to the final resting place, I was her baby brother. I would remain her baby brother until she took the very last breath. My mother never said my name again.

I have grown to accept her passing. To this very day, my mother is still teaching me about pain. I know that she is proud of me. She is proud of the man that I have become. I know that she is leading my cloud of witnesses. Every so often, I get a reminder that she is still alive and watching me from a different vantage point. She is sitting and watching me, the youngest of her eight children. And every so often, God uses her voice to utter a Divine Whisper to my spirit-self.

This is how pain works. It reaches to the deepest and most tender place within us, but the Divine Whisper will not allow it to establish residency there. We have to look for that which is familiar—the voice that we've known since before our first breath. This is the comfort that comes when we transcend the illusions that are embellished and manip-ulated by the author of chaos and confusion. When we push through the prodding of vulnerability, we become who we are destined to be.

Pain actually has a way of making us better. This is the natural essence of how the human truly deals with pain. The spirit-self leads us to the path of healing. It shows us the means for transcending those things that seem incredibly overwhelming at the time.

Like a mother's voice, the succulent stir of pain ironically calls and summons the greatest that is within us. If we are able to work through the pain, it can become a source of motivation, strength, and energetic direction like no other. Like fire, if we are able to harness the energy of pain, we learn how to capture an incredible resource for moving us in the direction of positivity—for moving us in the direction of our destiny.

Reflection Questions:

1. Describe what has been the greatest pain experienced by your physical-self.

2. What are the most common controlling tactics used by your ego-self to limit you?

3. What must you do to bring a greater sense of awareness and understanding of your ego-self?

4. What state of pain are you experiencing that is propelling you forward into a greater space of strength?

5. Imagine what it would feel like to harness the feelings of pain and translate those feelings into power.

   a. What are the steps of harnessing the feelings of pain?

   b. What must you do to translate the feelings of pain into power?

_____

_____

_____

_____

_____

_____

_____

_____

_____

_____

CHAPTER 6

BRAKING MY WAY TO
THE *NEXT* LEVEL

Most things are fairly easy to grasp on the surface. But the things that are really important require breadth, depth, and dimension. This is a basis of truth. For it is the truth that endures the rigors of time.

One of my favorite recreational endeavors is riding motorcycles. I ride a BMW K1200GT. I call it "The Beast." The bike is amazing. It has the power of a sport bike and the comforts of a touring bike. It takes a corner as smoothly as a breeze and powers through a straightaway with the torque of a race bike. I love riding this motorcycle. It creates escapism like nothing else. When I'm riding and singing inside of my helmet, I have my own Carnegie Hall showcase. There's nothing like it. The wind, the beams of a fresh morning sun, the calm of All floating down the highway. It feels like you're sitting still, while at the same time, it is as close as you can get to flying and still be connected to the earth.

One day, I pulled into the garage and parked "The Beast" after having been out for a couple of hours. Immediately after a ride, when I park I typically look the bike over to be certain that everything is in order so that when I'm ready to ride again, I jump on the bike and roll out. On this particular day, I noticed that there was leakage on the top part of the front forks of the motorcycle. The leakage was brake fluid. I knew that this was a job that needed the attention of professionals. The next week, I took the bike to the BMW dealership's service department. They assessed the entire situation and shared with me that the brake cables needed to be replaced. This is neither a simple nor cheap job. I decided that their expertise was not going to be an option—far too expensive. I decided to do the job myself. Now, one of the reasons that I bought the BMW motorcycle is because I really like riding the motorcycle, not working on it. At best, I am a novice at motorcycle repair—at the absolute best! Nonetheless, I have more time than money, so my garage became a shop.

The first thing I did was run a copy of the diagram from the owner's manual. I blew it up large enough for me to be able to see it in the faint lighting in the garage. Then the surgical procedure began. I started bleeding the brake lines. "Bleeding the brake lines," how ironic, I thought, that is exactly what I was feeling inside—like I was bleeding. Anyway, the first actual step was to remove a pin from under the engine and let every drop of brake fluid flow out of the bike and into a catch pan. As I sat studying the diagram and listening to the steady flow of brake fluid, I heard the daunting voice of the ego-self, "What are you doing?" it said. "You are so going to screw up your bike." I must admit, I paused and thought about what was happening. I couldn't think about it too long. I had to go on and start the disassembly.

Slowly and meticulously, I moved forward with the disassembly of my motorcycle. I removed parts of the faring and eventually the engine cover. I laid out each part that needed to come off based upon the diagram. The disassembly was one of the scariest moments throughout this process. To see "The Beast" open, vulnerable, and exposed, I couldn't help but feel a very odd sense of discomfort—some kind of fear. The garage seemed quieter than ever before. There were times during the disassembly when the ego-self began to dance. I felt as though the ego-self knew exactly what to say to get my fears and lack of confidence all stirred up. But I kept pushing forward. The experience was so intense that the level of focus nudged me closer to exhaustion with the turning of each screw, with the removal of each clamp and spring. Finally, according to the diagram, I had removed everything that needed to be removed in order to start the replacement of the braking cables. There it was, the intricate components of "The Beast" spread about on the floor of my garage. As I looked on, I started to see the parallel between the motorcycle and the real-life issues that rest just below the surface.

First of all, I had a new-found respect for the overall operation and performance of the motorcycle. I found myself appreciating the craftsmanship of the details. At its origin, somebody had the great idea of putting a motor and a seat on a small two-wheeled frame, and today we now have finely tuned machines capable of exceeding 100 miles per hour with the greatest of ease. The human starts off a bit slow, teetering and toddling along. As we—the human race—continue to grow and expand on our capacity, we continue to become capable of more. Most great things start with a thought. The thought becomes a desire. And the desire becomes an action or a series of actions. This pattern repeats itself until something breaks or a stimulant is introduced that shifts the pattern. The worn and broken brake cables on my motorcycle forced me to go beyond the surface to get to the root of the issue. So often in life, we have issues that present themselves, and we do not go beyond the surface to deal with them; instead, we compartmentalize them and move forward without a resolution. We store them away until something happens to trigger that which is unresolved. At some point, we have to go beyond the surface and get to the core of the real issues.

Second, as I looked at the parts on the floor, I gained a deeper understanding of each part's role in the operation of the motorcycle as a whole. It became clear to me that each piece had a unique and well-designed role for the motorcycle to operate successfully. All of the miles that I had ridden on "The Beast" would not have happened if it were not for every single part. As people, when we go beyond the surface and begin to explore the roles of each individual part that affects us, truth is revealed. Just as I had carefully and meticulously disassembled the pieces and parts of my motorcycle, we as human beings need to disassemble the things that are broken inside of us. The process of disassembly within itself creates a deeper knowledge base.

I had not begun to fix anything on the motorcycle; I had simply disassembled what needed attention—what was directly connected to the parts that were broken. This process increased my depth of knowledge and appreciation for the motorcycle.

As people, before we start trying to fix things inside of us, what might be gained from simply reflecting on the internal pieces and parts that make us who we are? Gaining a deeper understanding of them, even without resolve, provides an intrinsic reward. The more we study ourselves and gain a deeper understanding of who and what we are, the greater our capacity is to find resolve.

Finally, in looking at the parts on the floor of the garage, one more thing was revealed. The concept of "free will" bubbled up to the surface. I found myself looking at all that was before me and asking internally, "What can I do to add to the beauty and functioning of the bike?" You see, the process of disassembly created a space for me to add a little of my own personality to the bike.

In life, we are sometimes so overwhelmed by the things that are the reflection of our composition, and of our own making, through which we cannot see the windows of opportunity. We miss the opportunities to change our trajectory.

Our choices create a platform for our unique expressions. We create the situations that we face in life. When we disassemble the choices that we've made over time and search for collinearity of those choices and the resulting outcomes, we have to then own the entire equation. Owning our choices and outcomes propels us to a greater sense of clarity. It provides us with instructive data for things that are to come. What if we could take all of the choices that we've made and lay them out on the floor in the garage? What would we learn? Would we find opportunities to insert unique nuances to our internal composition? Back to the bike. …

My work for the day was complete. I identified the cables that needed to be replaced and placed the order to get them in hand. I also looked over the disassembled parts to see if they looked like the images in the diagram. The only things that appeared to be broken or worn were the brake cables and the fixtures that are used to connect them to the bike.

A couple of days later, I returned to the garage to continue the surgical procedure that was already underway. The new brake cables and clamps had arrived. Today would be the day of reassembly. The first step was to be certain that I had received the correct parts. As I began to lay out the new cables to confirm the size, the fit, and the location, it became clear that there were tools needed which I did not have. Off I went to the dealership, auto parts stores, and motorcycle specialty shops. My efforts were futile. I ended up ordering the tools from online sources. This was an unplanned, unanticipated delay. Four weeks later, I had everything that was needed to properly start the reassembly process.

I began by taking yarn and running it through all of the areas where the new cables would fit. This was to confirm, yet again, that everything that was needed for reassembly was present and ready to be connected. Surprisingly, the process of carefully connecting the new cables, clamps, and fixtures was pretty straightforward. The final step of resetting and properly calibrating the brakes required expertise that was beyond my skill set. So I called a friend of mine who is actually a motorcycle mechanic. He agreed to come over, bring his electronic devices, and guide me through the calibration process. The rest of the reassembly went fairly smoothly. I had the honor of tightening down the final screw-clamp. Stationary brake testing was next. Finally, we reached a critical moment—the road test.

I rolled the motorcycle out of the garage, turned it so that it faced the street, and, then, I mounted "The Beast." It actually felt different. I think that because I had worked on the bike, I gained a deeper understanding of the intricate workings of the bike. I now felt a greater sense of ownership. When I cranked the engine, I heard the familiar rhythmic putter that settled to a tempered speed authority, which made me fall in love with this particular motorcycle in the first place. The moment of the test ride was finally here. I would soon find out if I had fixed the brakes or if my frugal nature would end up costing me more money? Slowly, I eased off of the clutch and carefully coasted down the subtle slope of the driveway. The moment of truth had arrived. I engaged the brakes ... Oh my God! ... They worked.

I was so proud of myself. I had fixed the brakes on my BMW motorcycle. There was a tremendous sense of pride and fulfillment. That afternoon I must have ridden for four or five hours. There is a little lake close to my home. I stopped there and sat in the solitude of the lake, the cozy embrace of an afternoon breeze, and the nurturing glow of the Texas sun. What an amazing space for reflection.

As I sat, I found myself pondering the entire experience of replacing the brake cables. I looked at "The Beast." The glow of the newly installed orange cables popped out as though stepping forward for the eyes to behold. Seeing the contrast of the bright orange cables with bronze clamps and screws against the hue of the bikes' dark blue framework was quite cool. It set the bike apart from other bikes of its kind and caliber.

The bright orange cables, bronze clamps, and screws were actually a reflection of my free will—my means of expression being demonstrated on my motorcycle. They were visual reminders that the bike had been minimally customized to reflect a bit of my personality. Anyone who knows me would look at "The Beast" and would say, "Yep. That is Jerry's bike. There's the orange." The orange is my chosen color. I wear orange somewhere on my body every day. It is truly "my color." For me, the color orange represents a zeal for the gift of life. It goes deeper than that, but that is another book. Anyway, it was only fitting that there was a hint of orange on my motorcycle.

We all have our special set of affinities. We are all unique in our own right. And, if we pause long enough, we would soon discover that each human is so uniquely created that individual expression is an art form within itself. What happens if a person is strong enough to live their lives from this space—a space of freedom? Living from a place where the latitude of expression fosters new and unique perspectives on all aspects of life. The latitude of expression positions us to receive the profound uniqueness of every person that we encounter. How different might our lives be? The capacity to be internally, intrinsically, and uniquely rich in expression is a gift from God.

As I sat, I also thought about the process of discovering that I needed some additional tools. When I was doing the disassembly, my set of tools worked just fine, but when it was time to put "The Beast" back together, I realized that I needed more tools. Sometimes in this life's journey, we face situations that tell us with great intensity that more tools are needed. Regardless of where you come from, regardless of how much or how little you have, regardless of what others might suggest by way of unsolicited comments—the bottom line is that the individual has to identify when more tools are needed for them to go to the *Next Level*. After all don't we all want to go to the *Next Level*?

When we look at the journey of each person through life, there is tremendous diversity from person to person. We often feel that we have all the tools that are needed to move us forward. It is not until we sit still and look back at all of the contributing factors to our rich or impoverished current existence, and it is not until we look back that we realize that we could have done some things better. Choosing to get the tools needed to be better equipped to go forward in whatever aspects of our lives is truly a choice. The new tools or new skills reflect growth. It is never too late to choose to be better. Along the way, tools and skills that further develop who and what we are result in personal growth. They position us to do more, to be more, to respond to the calling on our lives. Failure to acquire the new tools puts us one step closer to death.

Finally, I decided to get back on "The Beast" and ride home. While riding home, it became clear to me that re-cabling the brakes on my motorcycle helped me to grow. My drive to save money by doing it myself really proved to be the catalyst to something much greater. The revelation that seeking a deeper understanding of something that I felt that I already knew about and something that I already had a deep appreciation for was but a mere brush of the surface.

When I saw the internal aspects of the braking system, I grew. When I pushed through the discomfort and lack of security about what I was trying to do, I grew. When I did the reading to ensure that I was ordering the right parts, I grew. When I faced the reality that I needed more tools, I grew. When I chose to seek help for the recalibration of the braking system, I grew.

The ride home was actually a celebration. As I made my way home, I realized that changing the brake cables on my motorcycle was a moment of transformation. For me, this process laid out a clear point of reference for recognizing the opportunities to go to the next level in so many other areas of my life. I realized that the space for transformation is constantly present. We just have to learn to see it. And, we have to be intentional about choosing it.

Remember, this chapter started with me saying that truth endures the rigors of time. The truth is that I love riding "The Beast" more now than ever before. I am so glad that my brake cables wore out. Doing the work myself took me to a whole new level as a motorcyclist. After that experience, I became a better rider. We all have to learn to see the opportunities for transformation. In order to go to the next level, we must operate in the space of truth. How different would our world be if we operated from this space? How different would it be if we looked for the opportunity to see and to speak to this same space—the space of freedom and truth—in other people? What if we all would speak from this higher space within? What if we all were to speak spirit to spirit?

Reflection Questions:

1. What is on your list of internal things that need to be disassembled?
2. What is the greatest fear of disassembly?
   a. What is the greatest gift of disassembly?
   b. In what way could reassembly transform you?
   c. Are you willing to be transformed?
   d. What are the three things that must happen for the disassembly and reassembly to facilitate the transformation that you desire?

_____

_____

_____

_____

_____

_____

_____

_____

_____

_____

_____

_____

_____

_____

_____

_____

_____

_____

_____

_____

_____

_____

_____

_____

_____

_____

_____

_____

_____

_____

_____

_____

_____

_____

_____

_____

CHAPTER 7

WHAT IF TODAY IS IT?

Transformation is about becoming aware of the physical-self; understanding the ploys, tactics, and strategies of the ego-self; and knowing and acting upon the dictates of the spirit-self. It is about taking all the unique attributes that God has given to you and repurposing them with a much clearer sense of purpose and greater value.

Transformation is uncomfortable; in fact, it is a process of discomfort. It is about total surrendering to God. When we do this, we are able to see from the God space, the sanctum sanctorum that is within each of us.

This allows us to recognize the best that is within others. This I call the "God window." When we are able to see the God window and speak through that window, with few words, we are able to touch the core of another person. And we speak clearly to the God spirit that is within them. This is the essence of transformation: living life in a way where we can see and speak to the best that each of us has to offer.

The heart is a funny thing. We all like to think that we know ourselves. We even have the audacity to think that we know others. The older I get, the more I realize how little I know of myself, let alone others.

Sometimes, we all need somebody to lean on. Ideally, we form relationships where the leaning is mutual. Ideally, the person—spouse, friend, partner, sibling, etc., makes the individual stronger and vice versa. Speaking spirit to spirit occurs in the deepest recesses of our souls—the sanctum sanctorum, the holy of holies, the God space that is inside each of us. This is pure truth. Sharing it in an unadulterated manner can be overwhelmingly intense, so the capacity to empathize where others are allows us to speak to the God space that is within them. This is speaking from spirit to spirit.

Frequently, we don't have enough strength to grow on our own. Remember, love is an action. People have to set the pace of transformation based on what God tells them individually. Remember, we are forever discerning the Divine Whisper from all of the other voices that speak in our head. The Divine Whisper speaks in a gentle space and with tremendous clarity. When we remove all of the distractions, clarity is revealed.

Sometimes, God puts people in the presence of others so that God can use them to speak to others. God knows what is ahead of each of us. God uses people to move the Divine plan forward. FEAR is false evidence appearing real. This is the slippery, slimy, elusive tempter. It is an illusion and it operates in the space of our thoughts. Truth endures the rigors of time. Stand in the strength of REAR, real evidence affirming reality. We all have databases of information, past experiences, previous situations, and deep-seated testimonies that speak to making it through, over, or around challenges that have presented themselves over the course of our life. This information is stored both in our head and our heart. We have a repository of instances when we thought that we couldn't make it, yet somehow we did. Fact-driven truths cancel the capacity of the evil one to use the illusions of fear to hold us hostage. Reality is that we all have the capacity to stand in the strength of truth.

The Four Disciplines of Intention are foundational practices that, over time, position us for being in alignment with God and for operating at our highest possible level in all aspects of our lives. The twenty-eight minutes of time invested yield a return that is beyond measure. The disciplines elevate our self-awareness, deepen our understanding, and instill a greater sense of knowing. This allows us to communicate in a way that is incredibly connectional. The outcomes of transformation may be observable in the sense that we listen with greater focus and we share with greater depth.

Because of the increase in life expectancy at older ages, people aged ninety years and older now compose 4.7 percent of the older population (age sixty-five years and older), as compared with only 2.8 percent in 1980. By 2050, this share is likely to reach 10 percent. It seems that if a person lives more than ninety years of age, they have lived a full and rich life. It is reasonable that they have consistently done some things correctly. No one is the judge, but everyone is a pupil. Longevity is a natural teacher.

Have you ever attended the funeral of a person older than ninety years? I know that at this point you're thinking, "What is wrong with this guy? He is always talking about death."

But seriously, is there really a clearer time in a person's life than when the journey is completed and the human stands at the crossroad of transition to the afterlife? From the first breath of this life, with every step that we take, we are one step closer to the ultimate destination. Rarely do we get up in the morning and start the monotonous routines of daily life thinking that today is the last day of my life here on earth. What if today is the very last day?

What if today is the very last day to go to school? What if today is the very last day to take the kids to school? What if today is the very last day to put gas in the car?

What if today is the very last day to go to the job? What if today is the very last day to kiss the spouse? What if today is the very last day to pack the lunch? What if today is the very last day to stand in front of the mirror and shave? What if today is the very last day to listen to that favorite song? What if today is the very last day to ride the motorcycle? What if today is the very last day to take a deep breath? What if today is the very last day to go to …?

What if today is the very last conversation with those who are dear to you. What if today is the very last day? What if today, it all ends—it's over? What if today, … this life concludes?

What would you do differently today? How would you speak to others? What would you speak about? Would you speak from a space of truth? What if you spoke from spirit to spirit, meaning what if you spoke from the space of the Divine Whisper that is inside of you to the Divine Whisper that is inside other people? What if you could get past the physical self and the ego-self? What if you spoke from the spirit-self for the entire day? How different would your day be? I dare you to try it.

There was a man named Curvis, who was approximately ninety-three years old and had died—transitioned from earth to heaven. In heaven, he was greeted by one of God's angels—the Tour Angel. The Tour Angel said to the man, "Welcome. I am your designated tour guide. We've been preparing for you for the last couple of days." He said, "I will be taking you to several places today so that you can get settled in for eternal life. We will start by walking down Main Street."

Curvis was completely smitten by everything he saw as they began to walk down Main Street. The street was made of gold. The brightness of the sun and the sheen of glistening bells accompanied by the courtship of the Harp Angel soothed his spirit. The man thought to himself, "Wow … So this is it. I made it. I am in heaven."

The Tour Angel showed him the well of cleansing. He said,

"This is the well of cleansing. You will only need to visit it once during eternal life. We'll stop and let you be dipped a little later today. No worries, it is just a formality. Everything here is sterile and clean beyond measure. Over there is the fountain of forgiveness. There is a line right now. God will allow you to pass through there if it is deemed that there are matters of unresolved forgiveness. Come this way."

As Curvis followed along, he thought, "Man, I should have given in and come on up here years ago. What was I thinking?" The Tour Angel said, "Come on, Curvis. You can walk faster. All pain has been removed from your entire body. Whatever limping you're doing is because of habit. I assure you that all pain has been removed." He stopped and instructed Curvis to stand up straight, relax his shoulders, make small circles with his head, and walk freely. Embrace the comfort of heaven—meaning embrace being in the presence of God. Curvis followed the instructions to the letter and was amazed that he was free of all pain. He said to the Tour Angel, "I feel so light!" This is amazing. "How long before I meet God?" "Be patient my brother" replied the Tour Angel, "You will see God soon."

They continued to walk to the end of Main Street. When they turned the corner, there was a table filled with fresh fruit and vegetables. Curvis could smell the aroma of fresh bread baking. He looked to the immediate right and there was a pool of pure water filled with the gift of life. The Tour Angel said:

> When you drink from this fountain and you will be reenergized for worship and glorification of God. You do realize that the great majority of your time here in heaven will be spent in worship and praise service. Sometimes, we get caught up in the moment, and the Holy Spirit takes us into a deeper state of worship. I tell you, it is easy to get dehydrated. So monitor yourself. Come and drink from this, the fountain of life.

As they continued to walk, John the Apostle was walking by. "Hello, sir," said the Tour Angel. "How are things in the mansion?" "All is well," said John. "Greetings, sir. You look like a newcomer." Yes, sir. I am," said Curvis. "Well, just know that heaven is now your new home. All that is before you is the blessing of God, our Savior. Enjoy! It gets better and better here every single day. Blessings," and John departed.

Curvis said, "Are you serious? That was John the Apostle?" "Yes," said the Tour Angel. "He moves around a lot. I see him almost every day." The Tour Angel began to slow down and look at the entrance way of several doors that were now directly in front of Curvis and him. "This is it. No, that is not it … Ok. Here it is. Come on, Curvis. I want you to look inside this room. Now, before I open the door, I need you to take a deep breath," said the Tour Angel. He touched the door, and the the door began to open slowly, "Behold the glory and splendor of God's blessings!" said the Tour Angel.

Curvis took two steps forward and entered the room. His face froze in a state of astonishment. The very first thing that he saw was his blanket. "Oh my God!" said Curvis. "That is my blanky. My grandmother knitted that for me when I was a baby. I kept it until I went to the first grade. I could not go to sleep without it. Finally, my mother told me, 'OK, Curvis. It is time to leave your blanky behind. You're a big boy now.' Man, I wondered what happened to this thing."

He turned to the left and saw his first bike. He exclaimed as he walked over, "It's my bike! Oh my God! How did you guys get this stuff! That was the very first bike that I every had." He ran over to it and jumped on, straddling the bike as if he was going to ride it. "I learned how to ride bicycles on this little blue bike. Boy did I have fun on this thing." Out of the corner of his eye, he saw a sweater with big red letters "LR" on it. He dismounted the bike, dropping it to the ground and moving with intention in the direction of the sweater. "That's my school sweater from Lincoln Road Elementary. That is where I went to school." He took the sweater in his hands, raised it up to his nose and smelled it. He said, "I used to wear this thing everywhere." And then, in a moment of complete awe, Curvis began to cry.

He walked forward slowly. "I cannot believe this is here. This thing changed the course of my life. I remember the day when Mr. Jones gave it to me." He wept as if having returned to adolescence. "This is the toolbox and all of the tools I received when I officially became a master carpenter. Oh my God, I was so very proud! This toolbox and the tools in it changed my life. This is what I used to build my house. These are the tools that I used to earn a living to take care of my family. This was my life—building stuff, working with wood." The Tour Angel said, "I'll give you some time. Enjoy."

Curvis continued to see things that were reminders of all of the milestones of his life. He was reunited with every single gift from God, at least all of the very special ones. In this room was the collection of blessings that God had given him over the course of his ninety plus years of life on earth. He reflected on each of them. When the Tour Angel returned, Curvis said, "This has been amazing. It is like a video of my whole life in this room. Will I be able to come back in here again?" The Tour Angel said, "No. There is not a need for you to come back here.

This was just a time and space for you to reflect on your life. The room that you were in is called the Room of Blessings. The purpose of the room is for you to see how good God was to you over the course of your earthly life. In that room was every tangible gift that God gave you. You will not need to come back here again. Remember, you are in heaven. You are now in the presence of God. There will not be a need for earthly reminders. That room was a sentimental reminder so that you could close the chapter on your earthly existence and embrace eternal life. As we walk on to our next stop, I challenge you to think about how good God had been to you. Follow me."

Curvis was filled with a mixture of emotions and feelings. His mind continued to reflect as they began walking to the next stop. A certain part of him was sad because it was so much fun to look back over his life and see all of the blessings, but at the same time, he was eager to see what was next. Curvis asked the Tour Angel, "What's next? Where are we going now?" The Tour Angel said, "Just follow me. I'm taking you to our next stop."

"Hello, ladies," said the Tour Angel. "Hi, Tour Angel. You are always busy. An Angel's work is never done, you know," said one of the ladies. "Yeah Tour Angel," said the other lady. "When was the last time that you took your wings off and sat still?" The Tour Angel replied, "Well, never." They all laughed. "You know our Master. Work. Work. Work. The work is never done. Besides, I love what I get to do so much that it doesn't feel like work." "And you're so good at it," said the lady

Tour Angel said, "Ladies, this is Curvis. He is getting checked in. Curvis, this is Ruth and Esther; on earth, they were incredible women of God. You read about them, right?"

Curvis could not speak. He nodded his head in agreement. Ruth said to him, "It is okay. Our labor was actually no different than yours. The only difference is that there was the man following us around writing about our stories." Esther commented, "Yes. I am familiar with your work. I love the way that you continued to come up with those funny little phrases to help people see God and understand God's word. I thought your approach was truly unique." Ruth chimed in, "Indeed, indeed. I can truly relate to your drive and your work ethic. Anyway, we won't keep you all any longer. Welcome to heaven, Curvis. We'll see you around; in fact, we'll save you a seat down front. Tour Angel, do you think that you guys will make it to the next worship?" "I think so," said the Tour Angel. "We'll see you both later."

As they walked away, Curvis said, "This is really going to take some getting used to." I couldn't find the words to even speak to the two of them. I think that I am overwhelmed." "Well, said the Tour Angel, "You will get used to it. It is overwhelming for most people when they first get here." The two continued to walk until reaching yet another door. As they stood in front of the door, the Tour Angel said to Curvis, "Well, we have arrived." Curvis asked, "Is this it? Am I now going to stand before God?" The Tour Angel said, "No. This is the final reference point regarding your life on earth, other than your conversation with the Master. I need for you to be intentional about paying attention when you enter this final room. So take a few deep breaths, center yourself, and just remember, this is your final reference point for your life on earth as a human. After this, well, I'll tell you where we're going after we leave this room."

Curvis did just as he'd been instructed. The Tour Angel opened the door, took a big step back, and said to Curvis, "Okay, sir. Go ahead and enter. Remember to breathe." Curvis entered the room and walked forward almost to the center of the room. He turned and looked to what seemed to be the south side of the room. Then he turned and looked westward. Slowly and with a slightly puzzled look on his face, he looked to the north. Finally, he looked to the east and said to the Tour Angel, "What is it? This room is full of stuff, but I don't recognize any of the things in here." The Tour Angel stared at him with a serious and slightly sad look on his face. "Why aren't you saying anything? What is it? What am I missing? Should any of this look familiar to me?"

An awkward silence filled the air. The Tour Angel didn't say a word. Curvis said, "Why aren't you saying anything. I'm sorry. Did I do something wrong. Please, Tour Angel. Tell me what I'm supposed to do."

The Tour Angel said to Curvis, "I want you to look around at the amazing things that are in this room."

"You're right," said Curvis. "There's a whole stack of money on that side. Boy, I could use that cash. Well, Wait a minute. Do we need money here in heaven? Look at that shiny sports car. I always wanted one of those. And look, there's a building with my name on on a huge billboard across the top of it. I always wanted to be in real estate." The Tour Angel said, "Exactly!"

Curvis thought, what does he mean? Finally, he stated with the sound of total confusion, "Exactly? What do you mean, exactly!" Tour Angel didn't say a word.

He stared at Curvis and he finally said,

"Curvis. Everything that you see in this room—and, just so that you understand, this one room is seven times the size of Cowboy stadium—I'll give you time, if you'd like, to walk around and see everything; but honestly, I really don't see the point. Curvis,… this room is your room of unclaimed blessings. In this room are all of the blessings that God had in store for you and you never claimed."

There was a long, painfully quiet pause, and the Tour Angel continued, "In this room is every gift that God had designated specifically for you, but you never claimed them. God wanted you to claim them, and you did not claim them. So now these items will go back into the inventory and will be designated for other people."

In speaking spirit to spirit, the dialogue is not solely about looking and finding the best in ourselves and looking and finding the best in others. It also includes speaking to the best in others, encouraging them, nurturing them. It is also about being able to get past yourself and being free to speak honestly and truthfully to God.

Be ye transformed. Speak spirit to spirit. And leave the room empty.

Reflection Questions:

1. How do you describe the sanctum sanctorum that is within you?
   a. What must you do to access this space within?
   b. What is the name of the voice that meets you there? Describe how this voice sounds. Describe the context necessary for you to have the greatest opportunity to clearly hear this voice.

2. What makes you insecure about speaking to others from this space?
   a. What must you do to gain the confidence to speak to others from this space?
   b. How might your speaking from this space affect others?
   c. What about speaking from this space allows you to be consistent?
   d. How does sharing from this space connect you to elements of time?
   e. What does your REAR reveal to you about sharing from this space?

3. What must happen for you to speak "truth" to others from a place of love?
   a. How might you benefit from consistently speaking from this space?
   b. Describe the traits or characteristics of what you see in others that inspires you to speak to them from this space.

4. What decisions must you make in order to "leave the room empty"?
   a. With whom will you share your decision?
   b. How might you ask them to help you be accountable?
   c. When will you start speaking spirit to spirit?

_____

_____

_____

_____

_____

_____

_____

_____

_____

_____

_____

_____

_____

_____

_____

_____

_____

_____

_____

_____

_____

_____

_____

_____

_____

_____

_____

_____

_____

_____

_____

_____

_____

_____

_____

_____

_____

_____

_____

_____

(Source: https://www.census.gov/newsroom/releases/archives/
aging_population/cb11-194.html. October 22, 2017. 9:12 a.m.)

ABOUT THE AUTHOR

D r. Roberson works extensively with professional athletes and entertainers. He is credited with elevating the performance of athletes in many different competitive arenas and of entertainers on numerous levels. His skillset and consistent genuine interest yield deep connections with these highly visible people. His interactive exercises and stimulating questions create conversations that are sometimes hard to describe by his clients, but the results are clear to those whom he coaches. His process of revealing what is within to empower that which is external has immediate positive impacts. The awareness and intention have been described as the cause agent for athletic prowess and deepened artistic expression.

As a master policy strategist and coach, Dr. Jerry has played an integral role in the enactment and the implementation of policy on the state and federal levels. His work continues in the maternal and child health disciplines as a high-performance program evaluator and project coach.

Jerry's formal education includes a doctorate of public health with two specializations—social and behavioral health, as well as health management and policy from the University of North Texas Health Science Center located in Fort Worth, Texas. He obtained a master of arts in communication studies with a concentration in film from Baylor University in Waco, Texas. His bachelor of arts in journalism was earned at Northwestern State University located in Natchitoches, Louisiana.

Dr. Jerry's spirituality and diverse background give him a unique perspective as he helps his clients achieve at their optimal level and live into the richness of their true selves.